Killing Time

A thriller

Richard Stockwell

Samuel French — London
New York - Toronto - Hollywood

KILLING TIME

Killing Time was first performed at the Theatre Royal, Windsor, on 5th August 1997. The cast was as follows:

Rick	Dennis Waterman
Jane	Glynis Barber

Director	**Roger Redfarn**
Designed by	**Simon Higlett**
Lighting by	**Nick Beadle**

COPYRIGHT INFORMATION

CHARACTERS

Rick, mid—late thirties
Jane, mid—late thirties

The action takes place in the living-room (with a kitchen area) of a well-to-do house

Time: the present, late afternoon

Samuel French is grateful to Charles Vance, Vice-Chairman of the Theatres Advisory Council, for the following information regarding the Firearms (Amendment) Bill:

"The Firearms (Amendment) Bill does not affect blank-firing pistols which are not readily convertible (i.e. those which do not require a Firearms Certificate). Among the reasons against imposing restrictions on such items is their use in theatre, cinema and television as a "safe" alternative to real guns.

The general prohibition on the possession of real hand-guns will apply to those used for theatrical purposes. It would clearly be anomalous to prohibit the use of those items for target shooting, but permit their use for purposes where a fully-working gun is not needed. As handguns will become "Section 5" prohibited weapons, they would fall under the same arrangements as at present apply to real machine guns. As you will know, there are companies which are authorised by the Secretary of State to supply such weapons for theatrical purposes.

The exemption under Section 12 of the Firearms Act 1968, whereby actors can use firearms without themselves having a Firearms Certificate, will remain in force".

Regulations apply to the United Kingdom only. Producers in other countries should refer to appropriate legislation.

ACT I

The living-room (with a kitchen area) of a pleasant, well-to-do house. Present day, late afternoon

One senses a leafy suburb outside. This house stands alone, back from the road. Perhaps we can see a tree or two through the kitchen window, which looks out towards the front of the house and the garden and street beyond. A door leads to the small entrance hall LC—there is a coat hook on the back of it. DS of the door is a small chair

The UL area of the stage is the kitchen area, not overly large but neatly laid out and well equipped. It is tidy, as though it has not been used for a while. A kitchen counter divides this area from the rest of the room. A TV is on the counter, also a pile of old newspapers. Also on the counter is an untidy length of wood. It has been broken off the front door frame, which is out of sight through the hall. The piece of wood has ragged pointed ends, and a couple of large nails protruding from it

The living-room is R. Through its windows R there is a glimpse of the garden, but the blinds are mostly down. In this area, just R of C, is a sofa and to the right of that, an armchair. Above the sofa is a standard lamp and next to this, facing US and out of the window, is a small wicker chair. There are spotlights on the walls. Long window sills provide stands for family photographs. In front of the sofa is a coffee table and on it a telephone and a notepad. There is a small dining table DL, with matching carvers around it. A briefcase, which is on the sofa, is the only sign of any recent human presence. There is a door to the garden UR

We hear a car pulling up over a gravel drive. Doors open and close. Footsteps. Two people walk past the living-room windows from R to L

We hear the front door pushed open and then the door to the hallway opens and Rick comes in. The years have not been kind and his face shows the hard passage of time. He is wearing a smart and functional business suit, more probably Marks and Spencer than Armani. He carries in his hand a supermarket carrier bag with some cans of beer in it and a few items of groceries

Rick handles the groceries carefully as though afraid he might break them and he has a purposeful way of moving which suggests a man of action. He is very polite to his guest and perhaps overly solicitous. He is, we feel, not used to entertaining but his hesitancy is not shyness, merely social uncertainty, and he is inclined to pull at his clothes as if they are uncomfortable—or perhaps just unfamiliar

Rick Here we are.

Behind him comes Jane. She is probably the same age as Rick but the years, her make-up, and the local hydro have proved kinder to her. By contrast her clothes are apparently casual but clearly expensive (Armani might well have done some business here). She wears a long coat of deceptively plain cut and, as she moves, the folds turn in a way that talks money. When she takes the coat off she is wearing a particularly striking pullover. One senses that she enjoys organising her appearance but also that the clothes are a costume that hide something. It could be vulnerability or it might be something else. She drops her car keys into her bag. As she comes in she turns and indicates the front door

Jane Shall I close the door?
Rick It doesn't shut properly.
Jane You went out when the door doesn't close properly?

Rick picks up the chunk of wood which is leaning against the inside door frame

Rick I've already been burgled. There's nothing to steal.
Jane What's that?
Rick Someone kicked the door in. This came off. TV, video, a bit of loose cash—that's what they're after. I figure they won't come back until the insurance claim's gone through.
Jane For the cash?
Rick What?
Jane (*indicating the TV*) They didn't get your TV.
Rick No, not this one. I think they were disturbed. They took my laptop.
Jane You should get it fixed.
Rick (*joking*) The laptop?
Jane The door.
Rick Yeah. Have a seat. Is it coffee or tea … or something stronger? Sorry, let me take your coat.
Jane Thanks.
Rick Great sweater.

Jane Thank you.

Rick Where do you find something like that?

Jane Marks and Sparks.

Rick I don't think so. (*He hangs her coat up on the hook behind the door*)

Jane Just a place I know.

Rick Expensive?

Jane Why, do you want one?

Rick No. Just curious, it makes an impression. So what was it going to be?

Jane Sorry?

Rick The drink.

Jane What time is it?

Rick (*smiling*) If you want a drink say so. There's no need to be embarrassed. I won't tell your friends that you were drinking at five o'clock.

Jane What are you having?

Rick A beer.

Jane goes to sit on the sofa. Rick nearly says something, but she sees the briefcase and moves towards the armchair instead

Jane Yes. I'll have one of those. Thank you.

Rick gets the beers out of the carrier bag

Nice house. Quiet?

Rick Fairly. It's nice to be back from the road.

Jane A bit of privacy.

Rick Yes. They aren't that cold. (*He hands her the beer still in the can*)

Jane is a little surprised to have the beer served this way. They hover uncomfortably near the kitchen area

Jane Thanks.

Pause. They drink their beers

It really is very kind…

Rick We've covered that. You don't need to thank me any more. You gave me a lift home. Call it quits.

Jane When I've repaid the money I'll call it quits.

Rick OK.

Pause

Jane (*laughing at herself*) It's so embarrassing. I mean it's bad enough on a normal day going to the checkout and digging for your cheque book and feeling everyone's eyes boring into you. As if none of them ever pay by cheque…

Rick I know.

Jane …and then today … the cashier's hand reaching out for money … I just wanted the earth to swallow me up. I was sure I had my purse with me.

Rick It's been nicked.

Jane I may have just left it at home.

Rick Don't always think the best. It's been nicked.

Jane Very optimistic!

Rick You should ring the bank. Cancel your cards. You can ring from here if you want.

Jane It's all right. I'll wait 'til I've checked at home. If I have lost it, Michael can sort it out with the bank.

Rick Michael's your husband.

Jane Mmm.

Slight pause

Rick Do you get on well?

Jane Yes, of course.

Rick He won't have a fit when you've lost your cards?

Jane No.

Pause

Yes, he'll have a fit.

Slight pause

He'll get over it.

Rick He looks after the money matters, does he?

Jane Meaning I'm the silly little woman who loses her purse and doesn't cancel her credit cards?

Rick I didn't mean that.

Jane I know what you meant. Just because I'm grateful for your baling me out doesn't mean I'm a soft touch.

Rick Of course not.

Slight pause

Jane Sorry. I suppose it must sound a bit like that.

Rick A bit.

Jane Michael does like to keep his hands on the money. He's always been…

The phone rings. Jane pauses politely to let Rick answer it. Rick initially stiffens up, then ignores it. They look at each other while the phone rings. At last…

Aren't you going to get that?
Rick No, I'll leave it.

The phone rings

Jane I couldn't bear that. Go ahead, take it, I don't mind.
Rick No. I don't want to.

The phone stops at last

Jane Won't that niggle away at you for the rest of the day? Wondering who it was, what did they want?
Rick No.
Jane It would me. I hate missing calls.

Slight pause

Rick You're not drinking your beer.
Jane Neither are you.
Rick It's too warm. Let's have something else. Gin and tonic?
Jane Go on, then.

He takes the beer away and starts searching for glasses, opening several different cupboards in the kitchen area

Rick So he can be a bit moody sometimes?
Jane Michael? I think it would be fair to say he's … well, unpredictable. Yes, more and more, actually… Are you all right?
Rick Just looking for the right glasses. Here they are. Sorry, your husband?
Jane Well he was always short tempered, but the last couple of months a few things have … gone badly for him and it has made him really irritable.

Rick finds the gin and is now looking through cupboards for tonic

Rick Really?
Jane I don't know. He doesn't seem to have had any bad luck before.
Rick Sorry?

Jane He doesn't seem to have had any bad luck before.
Rick Sorry, I was looking for the tonic. I lost the thread a moment.
Jane I don't think he knows how to deal with it.
Rick I know what you mean. I knew a guy once, everything always seemed to go right for him. Had a sort of golden touch. You couldn't imagine anything ever going badly. The problem is it made him arrogant. Untrustworthy. Here you are. (*He hands her a gin and tonic. It almost slips from his hands, spilling slightly*) I'm sorry.
Jane That's OK.
Rick Sorry. My hands let me down sometimes.
Jane Oh?
Rick My grip is unreliable.
Jane I'm sorry…
Rick It's nothing. An accident some time ago.
Jane What happened?

Pause

(*Getting out a cigarette*) Do you mind if I smoke?
Rick No, not at all.

Jane looks in her bag for a lighter. Rick produces some matches from his pocket

Jane Sorry, would you like one?
Rick (*lighting her cigarette*) I don't smoke. (*He sits down at the kitchen counter. He watches the match burn right through, grasping the other end of it so as to burn it out*)

Jane stares at this performance. Rick swivels the charred remains in his fingers then crunches them up, allowing the ash to sprinkle on to the floor

Jane (*trying to make light conversation*) You seem dextrous enough.
Rick I'd rather not talk about that…
Jane I don't mean to pry.
Rick …not until I know you better.
Jane If you know me better.

Slight pause

Rick You were talking about your husband's good fortune.

Slight pause

Jane Yes… Do you mind if I get some more ice? No, it's fine, I'll do it. Might get something right today… (*She goes over to the fridge and finds some ice*)

Pause. Jane looks around the room for inspiration for new conversation. She indicates the newspapers

Recycling?
Rick Yes.

She indicates a collage of family photographs on one of the kitchen cupboards

Jane Your family?
Rick Just photos.

Jane looks at other photos arranged around the room

Jane And those over there?
Rick The same.
Jane You don't want to talk about your family?
Rick There's nothing of interest I can remember about them.

Slight pause

Jane Where are you from?
Rick Croydon originally.
Jane Oh?
Rick (*smiling at a private joke*) But I've been in the West Country for a while.

Pause

You were telling me about your husband.
Jane You don't want to hear about that.
Rick But I do.
Jane What about him? (*She goes to sit on the sofa. She picks up the briefcase to make some room for herself*)
Rick Sorry, I'll take that. (*He quickly gathers up the briefcase and moves it to the dining table*)
Jane It's OK, there's plenty of room.
Rick It's my work, you see.
Jane I see.

Slight pause. Rick sits on one of the dining chairs

Rick You were saying your husband was very lucky.

Jane Well, yes.

Rick In what way?

Jane When I met Michael, he'd just inherited a lot of money from some distant aunt. Everything he did with it seemed to come good. Money makes money, doesn't it? So we got married and he started up his own company.

Rick What sort of business?

Jane Property development. M J Holdings.

Rick M J?

Jane (*embarrassed*) Michael and Jane Holdings. (*She laughs*) A bit cute, isn't it? Seemed romantic at the time. A bit silly when you think about it. Michael and Jane Holdings. (*She sobers up*) Should be J Holdings really.

Rick Oh?

Jane It's all in my name, you see. The company. Some sort of tax dodge, I think. I own the company, he runs it. Well, he tries.

Rick You sound less than impressed with your husband at the moment.

Jane We're having one of those … he's being … difficult.

Rick Bad tempered?

Jane He can be. He even lost his temper with our daughter this morning.

Rick Your daughter?

Jane Yes. Is there something wrong with that?

Rick No, I just didn't … you don't look like a mother.

Jane I hope that's a compliment.

Rick Certainly. How old is she?

Jane Sophie? She's six.

Rick Six? So she's your little darling.

Jane She's my little minx. I'm quite glad to see him angry with her sometimes. She needs to be put in her place.

Rick She's only six.

Jane Don't you start. She doesn't need another ally.

Rick Oh?

Jane Her grandmother dotes on her.

Rick Your mother?

Jane Michael's.

Rick She spoils her?

Jane Sophie's surrounded by people who fawn on her.

Rick Don't you?

Jane Of course, but someone has to discipline her.

Rick Where is she now?

Jane At a friend's house.

Rick What time are you supposed to pick her up?

Jane In a … hey, what's going on?

Rick Nothing, I'm just interested.

Jane Why?

Rick I'm just interested. That's all.

Slight pause

It's not every day I rescue damsels in distress from Tesco's.

Jane Some bloody damsel.

Rick One hell of a damsel.

Jane Are you going to turn into a smooth bastard now?

Rick Could be my lucky day.

Jane (*swigging at her drink*) I think I'd better be off.

Rick No, stay. I'm only trying to flatter you to get you to stay longer. At least finish your drink in peace.

Slight pause

Jane OK. But no passes. I really can't be bothered.

Rick OK. So you own the company?

Jane Yes.

Rick From what you've said you should fight back. Threaten to veto some of Michael's decisions. Bring him to heel.

Jane Who says he needs "bringing to heel"?

Rick You're telling me he doesn't?

Jane You are very sure of yourself, aren't you?

Rick When I know something is true there doesn't seem much point in ignoring it.

Jane So I should knock him into line.

Rick Yes.

Jane You haven't met him. (*She pauses slightly*) Besides, it's been a difficult time for him.

Rick You don't care about him enough to mind that he's had a bad time.

Jane Where do you get off telling me about Michael?

Rick (*sitting next to her on the sofa*) Look, you can leave any time you like, but sometimes it's easier to talk to strangers than it is to friends. I'm talking frankly. Why don't you? You've nothing to lose.

Jane What do you get out of it?

Rick (*shrugging*) Your company.

Jane You're pretty strange. You've just popped up to sort out my life, have you?

Rick Yes. So what's been the trouble? What's happening that makes him so particularly difficult? Was he in Lloyds or what?

Jane (*getting another cigarette*) No. Someone's got a grudge against him. They smashed up his car a couple of weeks ago. Broke all the windows.

Slashed the seats, the tyres, poured some kind of acid all over the paint work. It was a write-off.

Rick It happens.

Jane Then he tells me he's getting threatening notes. You know, very dramatic, cut out of newspaper and pasted up.

Rick What do they say?

Jane They're threats. Warnings about what's going to happen.

Rick Like the car.

Jane Yes.

Rick Police?

Jane Doesn't like them. He said he was going to hire a detective.

Rick Private eyes, eh? Have they got any leads?

Jane Don't ask me. They just take a hundred pounds a day and expenses as far as I can see and do nothing.

Rick Have they questioned you yet?

Jane Why would they want to question me?

Rick You're his wife. In my book that makes you a suspect.

Jane (*laughing*) You're the detective—right?

Rick (*laughing*) No.

Slight pause

So that's it? A couple of letters and a ruined car?

Jane No. They set fire to his office. Lots of papers and records destroyed. It'll cost them.

Rick It'll cost you.

Jane Yes, I suppose.

Rick No idea who it is?

Jane Michael thinks it's a bloke called John Finch.

Rick Who's he?

Jane Someone he sacked a while ago.

Rick A man with a grudge.

Jane Mmm.

Pause

I never met him.

Rick Don't you go into your office?

Jane No. I go to the AGM—that's about it.

Rick You should take more care of your money.

Jane I suppose.

Rick What's this John Finch got against Mike?

Jane Michael. He hates to be called Mike.

Rick Sounds like that's what we should call him, then.

Slight pause

So?
Jane Michael thought he had a hand in the till.
Rick So he kicked him out.
Jane Without a pay-off.
Rick Fair enough.
Jane Maybe, but he beat him up first.
Rick Michael beat him up? Why?
Jane He doesn't like to be cheated.
Rick Has he heard of the police?
Jane He said going to the police would be too much aggravation.
Rick I see.
Jane Mmm.
Rick Nasty.
Jane Yes.
Rick Horrid for you.
Jane Mmm.
Rick But that's not the whole story, is it?

Pause. After a while, Jane begins to weep. Rick moves over to her

I'm sorry. I shouldn't have been so nosy. I shouldn't…
Jane No, I'm sorry. I shouldn't have burdened you with all this. It isn't fair.
I'll leave you alone. (*She gets up to go*)
Rick Don't go. You can't go out like that; here, settle down.

Jane sits again. Rick collects a paper towel from the kitchen and hands it to her

Wipe your eyes. Another drink?
Jane No, thanks. I'm sorry.
Rick Not at all.
Jane I've been a nuisance for you. First you pay for my shopping and now
I throw all this rubbish at you.
Rick I asked for it. Anyway it'll settle down. Finch's probably had enough.
That'll be the end of it.

Pause

Jane I don't think so.
Rick Oh?
Jane It's… (*She rises and walks round the living-room. She is still fighting
against tears*)

At the moment she crosses, he leans over and takes something from her bag and puts it in his pocket

No, that's enough of my troubles. Your turn. You talk to me. Tell me about Rick. (*She goes to pick up a photograph*)

He speaks, distracting her

Rick Rick? What you see is what you get. You probably know more about me now than you want to.

Jane Come on, talk to me, you've heard about my insane life, how about your insane life?

Rick Who says it's insane?

Jane I'm just being flattering.

Rick Oh? Thank you.

Jane Well?

Rick I can't just explain myself like that. What's to tell?

Jane What do you do?

Rick Will that define me?

Jane It'd be a start.

Rick I'm a head hunter.

Jane Really?

Rick Really. I've been out of work for a while.

Jane You need to be hunted.

Rick (*smiling*) No.

Jane You work in the city?

Rick Not often.

Jane I thought that was where the head hunters hung out.

Rick Oh, I see. No, I'm not that sort of head hunter.

Jane What sort are you?

Rick I put people together for jobs.

Jane Do you like it?

Rick I did. Trouble is it all depends on trust. Someone lets you down, it all goes wrong. You can end up paying for years.

Jane Are you married?

Rick No.

Jane (*taking in the family photographs*) Really no. Or "No until I see how I get on with this conversation".

Rick Really no.

Jane You wouldn't lie to me.

Rick I haven't yet.

Pause

Jane You know what the next question is, don't you?
Rick Girlfriend?
Jane Yes!
Rick No.
Jane Who's this then? (*She shows him the picture she picked up earlier*)
Rick How should I know?
Jane They are your photos.
Rick No.

Slight pause

   I rent the house fully furnished.
Jane With photographs?

Rick shrugs

   So do you have a girlfriend?
Rick No.
Jane What, never!
Rick Not at the moment. Not for ten years.

Pause

Jane You're a good-looking bloke.
Rick Thank you.
Jane You're not gay?
Rick No.
Jane Ten years is a long time.
Rick Yes.
Jane Am I going to regret asking about this?
Rick I don't know.
Jane Why?

Pause

   You live alone?
Rick I do now.
Jane Do you like it?
Rick (*sitting next to her*) Sometimes. How long have you been married?
Jane Seven years. Don't change the subject.
Rick Were you in love with him?
Jane I don't want to talk about that. Anyway, it's your turn.
Rick Who said anything about turns? Why did you marry him?

Jane He was rich.

Rick Oh, come on. Did you love him?

Jane Yes, I did.

Rick Really?

Jane He's got his good points.

Rick I see.

Jane Are you celibate?

Rick Not by choice. How can you have loved him?

Jane Anyone can love anyone. You never been in love?

Rick Not yet. You mean he's changed?

Jane Not really, I can just see through him now. You're meant to tell me about you.

Rick Really.

Jane Ten years is a long time. Then suddenly you make a pass at a married woman in a supermarket.

Rick I didn't make a pass. I paid your shopping bill.

Jane Then you brought me back here.

Rick You brought me.

Jane You called me a damsel.

Rick You called me a good-looking bloke.

Jane Do you find me attractive?

Rick Do you want me to prove it?

Jane I don't know yet.

Rick Some things you don't forget in ten years.

Jane So tell me your secret.

Rick What secret?

Jane Whatever it is you're trying not to tell me.

Rick I'm answering your questions…

Jane Carefully. All I really know about you is you like flirting.

Rick In the right company.

Jane Tell me.

Pause

Rick It's a pity.

Jane What?

Rick lights another match. He repeats the performance, but they talk over it

Rick All the dead ends.

Jane I suppose we don't need to know everything about each other.

Rick No. But I want to know everything about you.

Jane You can't expect everything for nothing.

Rick What upset you just now?
Jane I don't think it's any of your business.
Rick I want to help.
Jane Is this your way of making a pass?
Rick It's one way of making a pass.
Jane Let's talk about something else.
Rick Jane. You and I have no past together. I'm the perfect person to talk to.
   I won't judge you. You should let it all out. Talk it through.
Jane What about you?
Rick What about me?
Jane You haven't told me all you could. You're holding back.
Rick I'll tell it to you.
Jane Do I want to know?
Rick I don't know. But I'll tell you anyway.
Jane This is weird.
Rick Yes. Tell me what else happened to Michael.

The phone rings. Rick freezes up. Jane at first makes no sign of being conscious of it. She doesn't reply to Rick's words because she is expecting Rick to answer the phone. Pause while it rings

   What else happened?
Jane Aren't you going to answer the phone?
Rick No, let it ring.

Jane laughs, and as she speaks, she picks up the phone, starting to hand it to Rick

Jane You'll lose all your friends if you don't answer your calls…

Rick jumps over and roughly wrenches the receiver away from her

Rick What are you doing?
Jane Ow! (*She holds her wrist*)

Rick listens to the phone for a moment, then slowly hangs up without speaking

   What the hell did you do that for? I only picked up the phone.
Rick It's my phone.
Jane There's no need to break my arm.
Rick I didn't want to take the call.
Jane You hurt me.
Rick You answered my phone.

Jane I didn't mean any harm by it.
Rick And I didn't mean to hurt you.
Jane It's time I left.
Rick (*quickly*) No. No.
Jane I think it would be best.
Rick Please stay.
Jane No, it was rude of me to stay so long.
Rick No. I asked you to.
Jane I know, but…
Rick I'm sorry if I was a bit rough.

Jane begins to make her way out

Jane It doesn't matter.
Rick It does. I get nervous about my work. There are some people I don't want to speak to at the moment.
Jane So you're avoiding your calls.
Rick Yes.
Jane You can't do business if you won't answer your calls.

Slight pause

You owe them money?
Rick No.
Jane I'm being nosy again.
Rick That's OK. Look, I'm sorry about your arm. At least stay and finish your drink. I didn't mean to hurt you.
Jane You startled me.
Rick I'm sorry, I was anxious about the call.
Jane You should have said.
Rick I know, please stay.
Jane I'll just finish my drink.
Rick Thank you. Listen, you must be hungry. Can I get you anything? There must be some food here somewhere. (*He moves towards the kitchen area*) I bought some crisps. Or did you want something more substantial?
Jane (*more relaxed*) You don't give in easily.
Rick I don't give in at all. Come on, have something.
Jane OK.

Rick opens some cupboards ineffectually

Rick I'm sorry about your arm. Do you want some ice or something?
Jane Save it for the gin and tonics.
Rick It's OK?

Jane It's OK. It was the surprise as much as anything.

Slight pause

Rick I'm glad you're staying. (*He starts putting various tins out on to the work surface*)

Jane In one sense I shouldn't be here at all, but you were a breath of air after all the trouble with Michael. It's nice to be able to talk. Look, I don't want to spoil this, but I do feel a bit vulnerable. That was all rather familiar.

Rick With the phone, you mean?

Jane Yes.

Rick Like Michael?

Jane Yes.

Rick I'm not like him.

Jane Well… I've told you so much about myself and I know nothing about you. Hardly surprising you frightened me.

Rick No.

Jane Where's that snack?

Rick (*referring to the tins*) I don't know what all this is but you're very welcome to it.

Jane laughs

Jane You never heard of fresh food?

Rick I'm used to cans.

Jane You don't look like you're used to looking after yourself.

Rick I live out of cans.

Jane Maybe you should let me forage for myself, you don't look too comfortable in the kitchen.

Rick No.

Jane looks in the bag of groceries

Jane Spaghetti hoops, spring onion crisps, shoe polish…

She holds up a hammer

I didn't know they sold hammers at Tesco.

Rick (*sharply*) I'll take that. Sorry. (*He takes it rather swiftly*)

Jane considers him a moment

Jane Calm down. I'm not going to hurt your hammer. I'm more interested in your catering than your carpentry.

Rick Sorry. No, Tesco's don't sell hammers. I got it from Homebase across
the way.
Jane (*smiling*) You really know how to look after yourself, don't you?
Rick (*flirting*) My mind wasn't on my shopping.

*Jane looks at him for a short moment, then resumes her search, looking in
the fridge*

Jane (*finding cheese*) Cheese! Crackers?

Rick shrugs

What do you eat your cheese with?
Rick Bread.
Jane Too stodgy. (*She sees some olives in the fridge*) Olives. I love olives.
You don't mind? (*She sees a tin of biscuits on the counter*) And biscuits.

*Rick shakes his head. Jane busies herself with making up some cheese and
biscuits*

You make strong gins.
Rick (*coming over to her*) You need a top-up?
Jane No. I've got the nibbles. It's hot in here. You should turn your central
heating down. (*She takes her jumper off*)
Rick Let me take that.
Jane Thanks.

Rick takes it and tosses it on to one of the dining chairs

Hey! Careful.
Rick What?
Jane Don't just screw it up and throw it away.
Rick Sorry.
Jane That's six hundred pounds worth of sweater.
Rick You're kidding!
Jane Never over money.

Rick goes and picks up the jumper reverently

Rick Why so much?
Jane Don't you like it?
Rick I think it's great, but six hundred quid…
Jane It's a one-off. That's why you pay so much, so they won't produce
another to the same design.

Rick I don't suppose you bump into too many of these in Tesco.
Jane None.
Rick I'll give it a chair all of its own.

He hangs the sweater over the chair by the hall door. During the following exchange, Jane continues to prepare her snack

Jane You'll have to handle me with more respect!
Rick I'll handle your clothes with respect.
Jane Just my clothes?
Rick It's all I've had my hands on.
Jane I should think so.
Rick No, I should think so.
Jane Travel hopefully…
Rick So there's hope?
Jane There's always hope.

Pause

I'm a bit of a cheese fiend. Would you like some?

Rick shakes his head

I was pleased when you accepted a lift. I wanted to … talk to you. I was so grateful after all the embarrassment. I was surprised when you said yes.
Rick Why?
Jane It's strange that you don't have a car.
Rick I have a car.
Jane You walked to the supermarket?
Rick No, I left it at Tesco's. I fancied a lift. (*He makes for the sofa*)

Jane laughs. Rick laughs too and sits

Jane That's nice. I'm glad, otherwise this would have been just a forgotten little incident. I mean we'd have gone our separate ways, I'd have sent you the money and that would have been that.

Rick nods

But … this is nice.

Pause

I was grateful … no, not for the money … though of course I am thankful for that too, I just was pleased to have a reason not to go back home. Straight away, I mean. There's lots here, you might as well have one. (*She passes a biscuit with some cheese on it to Rick*)

Rick OK. (*He puts his biscuit on the arm of the sofa and doesn't eat it*)

Pause

Jane (*preparing another snack*) You're right. I haven't talked to anyone and it all just builds up. The last week has been awful. Michael's been unbearable since the notes started. He's got very irritable and he shouts a lot. Then when he gets in a temper, Sophie cries a lot. The car ... when the office went, he came home in a blind rage. He charged round the house looking for an excuse to blame something on me, so he could hit me. It was just a shirt I'd left on a radiator but he slapped me. "You think we live in a slum," he said and then... (*The snack finished, she walks over to the dining table to put the plate down and eat. The briefcase is in her way and she goes to lift it*)

Rick (*snapping*) Please don't keep touching that.

Jane I'm just making room.

Rick takes the case from her. He puts it over by the armchair

Rick I'm sorry. It's important work. I worry about it.

Jane Is it fragile?

Rick You were saying?

Jane I've forgotten.

Rick Your husband's short temper.

Jane Is not unique. You run on a short fuse.

Rick Yes, I know. I'm sorry.

Jane (*sitting at the dining table*) It's all right, I'm used to it. Michael would have killed me for just looking at his bloody briefcase.

Rick How do you cope with that?

Jane I've got used to it. I know ... or I thought I knew how to deal with it. You know, when to stand back and let him fume. I feel trapped in the house, like a hostage. Just me and Sophie—and I feel like Sophie blames me. Somehow she thinks it's my fault that Daddy's angry all the time. He's driving her away from me. I never know when he'll come home, and if he does, what mood he will be in. He'll be nice to Sophie and then be mad at me. Then this last week with ... with the police.

Rick Police?

Pause

Jane I didn't even know. I thought she was, well she was my friend. But they'd been … for years. The whole stupid marriage a sham. All the money pointless, he'd been sleeping with that … cow.

Rick Who?

Jane Tracey. She's the accountant.

Rick How did you find out?

Jane The police told me.

Rick Oh?

Jane I'd been out in the garden. Just watering a few plants, being the perfect wife, keeping the family nest going. They arrived. Said they wanted to speak to Michael. I told them he was at work but they said they'd come from there. I asked them what the matter was. They told me Tracey'd been murdered.

Rick I'm sorry.

Jane (*snapping*) Don't be! They said they needed to talk to Michael and did I know he'd been sleeping with her. I swear I didn't know. I mean it's always the wife who finds out last, isn't it? I thought he was faithful to me. I really thought so, but then someone killed her.

Rick Do they know who?

Jane I think the police suspect Michael.

Rick What do you think?

Jane Well no, I can't believe it.

Rick So why do the police think it?

Jane It seems he'd slapped her about occasionally too, and she confided in one of her friends.

Rick So he's violent to everyone he knows, but you don't think it could be him.

Jane No! I'm sure it couldn't.

Rick You were sure he was faithful to you.

Jane Stop it.

Rick How can you be so sure it wasn't him?

Jane I don't know. I don't know anymore. There I was, fairly happy, making the best of it all. I have money … friends… I thought I could cope with him. I was secure in my ignorance and then all this comes along. How should I know if he killed the bitch? They deserve each other.

Pause

During the following speech, Rick comes round the back of Jane's chair and talks down to her from behind

Rick I understand. You feel a need for vengeance, don't you? You want to hit back. You want to feel compassion for her because she's dead but you only feel anger. She's lying on bloody sheets and you feel guilty about it

all. Don't. Why should you feel guilty? They betrayed you, but she's dead.
Stand up to the son of a bitch. Fight back.

Pause. Jane has recovered somewhat

Jane Fight back?
Rick Yes. Hard.
Jane How tough do you think I am?
Rick Tough enough. You're still there.
Jane So what are you saying I should do?
Rick Stand up to him.
Jane You mean I should laugh in their faces?
Rick Well, his anyway. I don't suppose she'd notice.
Jane (*shocked*) Jesus Christ! Was that a joke?
Rick Well, you aren't laughing.
Jane Strange advice.
Rick I know what I'm talking about. It's good advice. Will you take it?
Jane I don't know.
Rick I think we need another drink.

Jane nods. He goes to fix the drinks. She wanders up into the living-room

I'm sorry, I shouldn't have pressed you so hard. No wonder you don't want
to go back to him.
Jane Yeah, well…
Rick Do you mind?
Jane I'm sorry?
Rick Now you've told me.
Jane No. You were right. It's good to talk about it. Kind of healing.
Rick Cathartic.
Jane If you say so.
Rick I do. Your drink.
Jane Thanks.

Pause. They sit on the sofa

So?
Rick Hmm?
Jane You should eat something.
Rick I'm not hungry.
Jane Don't you want that biscuit?
Rick No.
Jane Do you mind if… I can't drink without eating. (*She leans across him
and takes his biscuit and cheese*) I mean, after a couple of gins… (*She eats*)

They are very close

Rick And some warm beer.
Jane I can handle it.
Rick You should be careful.
Jane Why?
Rick I got into trouble for saying that.
Jane What?
Rick I can handle it.
Jane I meant something else.
Rick Pity.

Pause. In spite of his words, he doesn't respond to this advance of hers and after a while the sexual provocation seems foolish to her. She edges away from him

Jane Do you want me to go?
Rick No.
Jane (*indicating his briefcase*) I thought … your work.
Rick No, I'll get to that later.
Jane What's your dark secret?
Rick Dark enough.
Jane Well?
Rick I'm loath to tell you.
Jane It can't be worse than what I've just told you.
Rick About Tracey? I saw all that on the news. I read the lurid details in the press. So I sort of knew the story already, I just didn't realize it was part of your story, so to speak.
Jane I hardly realize it myself.
Rick Strange business.
Jane Tell me.
Rick Secrets exchange?
Jane Mmm.
Rick I'm frightened to.
Jane Why?
Rick You'll think differently of me.
Jane But not necessarily worse.
Rick Oh, I think so.
Jane That bad? You'll have to tell me now because not knowing is weird, and besides, you promised.
Rick (*with a smile*) Did I? Yes, I did. I nearly told you earlier. When you said I was a good-looking bloke. I suppose it gave me confidence. Then when I said I hadn't … had a girlfriend for ten years.

Slight pause

...I thought you'd guess. I've been in Dartmoor for the last ten years.

Long pause. He sits quietly watching her. Jane is at first embarrassed, then slightly scared. She starts drinking her drink in quick sips as if she's trying to finish it quickly

Jane Dartmoor Prison?
Rick Shocking, eh?
Jane Well...
Rick I'm the same person who you spoke to before you knew.
Jane Oh, yes. I'm sure ... it's not something... I don't mind. I mean it doesn't matter at all. You've... I mean that's over, I'm sure ... isn't it?
Rick You mean I've "paid my debt to society".
Jane Quite.
Rick Yes.

Pause

More gin?
Jane No, I ought to get off.
Rick Pity.
Jane Why?
Rick I hoped that might interest you. You told me all your little dark secrets. I told you my big one.
Jane (*getting up*) Well... I've got to go...
Rick (*getting up*) So that's it, hurry home to your unfaithful husband. Send a discreet cheque to me with a one line note of thanks and thank God you didn't get any further involved.
Jane Not at all... Look, Rick, you're a nice bloke, but I think my life is complicated enough at the moment...
Rick Without fraternising with a criminal.
Jane We've never met before and you have to admit that all this is a bit strange...
Rick Fancy drinking gin and tonic with a criminal.
Jane I'm sorry you feel that way about it. It isn't that, I just think I've outstayed my welcome.
Rick Come on, honesty is the order of the day. What is so wrong with talking to an ex-convict? Why are you so bloody self-righteous all of a sudden? Your husband is being questioned by the police for murder and you are worrying about talking to me because I was inside for a while. You don't even know what I was in for.

Jane Yes, well, I'm sorry. I really must go.

Rick What about my advice?

Jane What?

Rick My advice. How to handle Michael.

Jane I shouldn't have told you all that.

Rick Stay a bit longer. This has to be more interesting than going back to him.

Jane No...

Rick Tell me this, has he got an alibi? Where was he at the time of the murder? Jane? Do you know? Perhaps he was with you? Perhaps he's asked you to tell the police that he was with you?

Jane How...?

Rick Aha! He has asked you for an alibi. You don't know what to do, do you? Is he just scared because the police keep hassling him, or did he really do it? You don't know, do you? Perhaps he's really a killer. You don't want to believe that, though, do you? Even though you hate him, even though he slaps you around a bit, even though he was screwing Tracey Munton, you don't want the man you've lived with for seven years to turn out to be a murderer, do you?

Jane You bastard!

Rick Getting warm, am I?

Jane Fuck you! (*She starts to go*)

Rick follows Jane. She opens the door, he slams it shut. He turns the key and puts it in his pocket

Rick Getting warm, am I? Who killed Tracey Munton? Was it Michael?

Jane Let me out of here.

Rick No.

Jane Get out the way.

Rick No.

She tries to walk round him, but he won't let her

Jane I'll start screaming.

Rick I thought your life was complicated enough already.

Jane Please let me out. (*She turns away and her hand reaches into her handbag*)

Rick No.

Jane whips round

Jane Then take this...

In her hand is an aerosol. She tries to squirt it into his face but he is too quick

*for her. He grabs her hand and it sprays harmlessly away from him. He spins
her round and throws her down into the sofa. Rick now has the spray in his
hand. She is shaken. He stands over her, very close*

Rick Jesus Christ, this is mace! You could've blinded me. I may have been
inside for a while, but isn't this stuff illegal?

*Jane looks scared and says nothing. She scurries behind the armchair for
protection, leaving her coat and bag on the sofa. Rick tries to lower the
temperature*

Let's calm down. I only want to talk to you. I'm interested in you. I just
wanted you to stay.
Jane It doesn't look like I have a choice.
Rick I am sorry about that. But you pulled this on me. (*He puts the mace on
the sideboard*) You have to admit you were enjoying talking to me.

Pause

Weren't you?

Pause

Weren't you?
Jane Yes.
Rick But you have to admit that you stayed on longer than politeness
required because you thought it was preferable to going home to your
husband who, by the sound of it, might knock you about because someone
else is knocking him about, or perhaps might lose his cool and murder you
the way he killed his mistress.
Jane Looks like I was wrong.
Rick Eh?
Jane You're worse than he is.
Rick Perhaps.

Long pause. Rick takes the glasses and tops them up

I know you shouldn't as you're driving. But what the hell, we're all crooks
together here, aren't we? (*He hands her a drink*)
Jane You didn't get ten years for drunken driving.
Rick No.
Jane So? You're obviously itching to tell me.
Rick No, Jane, you're wrong, I'm not. In fact, one of the first things you learn

in the nick is not to ask people what they're in for. Some don't mind, but others can get a little anxious.

Jane You don't mind.

Rick What makes you say that?

Jane "When I know something is true there doesn't seem much point in ignoring it."

Rick Touché.

Jane So?

Rick (*sitting on the arm of the sofa, next to her*) Doesn't mean I wouldn't enjoy you finding out.

Pause

Jane OK. I suppose you won't let me go 'til I've played this game, right? (*She pauses*) Kidnapping? (*She pauses*) Embezzlement?

Rick indicates she's getting warmer

Bank robber? (*She pauses*) Tinker, tailor, soldier, sailor, I don't know, and I don't suppose I want to know.

Rick Come on, Jane, think. You've had some clues.

Jane You were sent away for ten years.

Rick Yes.

Jane You said you hadn't lied to me.

Rick Aaah!

Jane Unless that was a lie.

Rick Hmm.

Jane You said you were a head hunter.

Rick Yes.

Jane You were leading a "gang".

Rick Yes.

Jane So you're Moriarty, and Sherlock Holmes put you away for ten years. Do we have to play games? (*She goes to pick up her coat and bag from the sofa*)

Rick hurries ahead of her and moves them away across the room out of her reach

Rick I'm sorry. I developed a taste for games. All that spare time, you see. Banged up. Haven't you heard how bad it is? Three to a cell sometimes for hours on end. You have to try and while away the hours. Killing time. Games are good. Sometimes friendly games, sometimes private games, sometimes...

Jane …malicious games. Can I go, please? I'm sorry, but I'm not that good at playing games.

Pause

Please, Rick. I'm sorry I was rude about your criminal record.
Rick Armed robbery.
Jane Oh, perfect. Armed robbery?
Rick Yes.
Jane I'm meant to be pleased to hear that?
Rick Why not? It's interesting work. Not nine to five…
Jane I'm being held hostage by a convicted thug!
Rick Ex-convicted. I've got a clean sheet. A new start. My parole officer thinks he can get me a job with the Post Office.
Jane (*with a short dry laugh*) The Post Office! Shouldn't you be holding them up.
Rick You shouldn't underestimate the subtlety of my work.
Jane Subtlety!
Rick Yes, sounds silly, I know. But it's a tricky business. (*He becomes quite expansive walking round the room*) You've got to find the right job, choose the right people for that job. Compile a team.
Jane Management skills?
Rick Are you teasing me?
Jane Teasing!
Rick This is what I do.
Jane Everyone should be proud of their work.
Rick (*losing it slightly and shouting into her face*) Dead right, Jane. Dead fucking right and don't you forget it.
Jane (*carefully*) I'll try and remember.
Rick People admire armed robbers. Look at Ronnie Biggs.
Jane Don't mention his name to the Post Office.
Rick Are you taking this seriously?
Jane You were talking about subtlety.
Rick Yes. You don't want to go around shooting people. You don't want to shoot anyone. The police tend to try harder if you kill people.
Jane All right, head hunter, how do you compile your team?
Rick What's the job?
Jane Your last one.

Slight pause

Rick Security van.
Jane Right.
Rick Four men. Manager. Inside man. Hard man. Driver.

Jane Manager is you, of course. Hard man, he shoots people?

Rick Hardest job. Looks like a lunatic, frightens the shit out of everyone, but doesn't shoot anyone.

Jane The driver is obviously your getaway. The inside man works for the security company?

Rick Of course.

Jane So?

Rick So we knew the route of the van. Rammed it with a Land Rover, cut our way in with chain-saws. Shouted a lot and ran off with about four hundred thousand pounds.

Jane laughs

What?

Jane Subtlety!

Rick It worked.

Jane Except for the ten years.

Rick Yes.

Jane I suppose it would be impolite to ask how you got caught?

Rick You're learning.

Jane Do I have to guess, or are you just not going to tell me?

Rick We'll see.

Jane Another game.

Rick So what do you think?

Jane I think it was the crime of the century.

Rick Don't patronise me!

Pause

Why did your husband kill his mistress?

Jane He didn't.

Rick Why do you say that?

Jane Because you did.

Rick I did?

Jane Yes.

Rick You'll have to excuse me, Jane, but this comes as a bit of a shock to me. Why would I kill Tracey?

Jane You know too much about it all.

Rick It was in the newspapers. Besides, you've told me everything about it.

Jane I hardly told you anything. You're too interested in it all.

Rick Professional interest?

Jane So why did you kill her?

Rick I didn't.

Jane Oh?

Rick It's a bit of a coincidence, don't you think? Kill woman—for motive
unknown, while on parole—then happen to bump into the wife of the dead
woman's lover. Pay her grocery bill and pour gin and tonic down her.

Pause

A bit bloody improbable, don't you think?
Jane So why am I still here?

Pause

This is part of your game?

Pause

Look, are you dangerous?
Rick Seems a strange question to ask someone who has just told you he spent
ten years inside for armed robbery. What does it mean?
Jane Just what it says, are you dangerous?
Rick Of course I'm dangerous. Lots of things are dangerous, Jane. It doesn't
mean they aren't good or useful.

Pause

A car is dangerous, but you can use it to get around the place. Your husband
is dangerous, but he pays for your nice clothes. A knife is dangerous, but
it cuts cheese. And you, Jane, you are dangerous because you carry this
around in your handbag… (*He picks up the mace and moves it to the dining
table*)
Jane It's for self-defence.
Rick Of course.
Jane I've never used it before.
Rick I'm honoured. Ever been tempted to use it on Michael?
Jane What are you getting at?
Rick Ever been tempted to use it on Michael?
Jane All the bloody time.
Rick How often does he hit you?
Jane Often enough.
Rick At all would be often enough.
Jane Every Tuesday and Friday and twice on Sunday. What kind of question
is that?
Rick We're learning about each other. We ask each other questions, we get
to know each other.

Jane You ask questions, I answer them. You know a lot about me. Why do we need to get to know each other?

Rick (*sharply*) Why not? I don't have many friends.

Jane Is this lonely hearts?

Rick Yes. I'm lonely. I'm single. I haven't had sex for over ten years.

Jane I'm not available.

Rick That's not the message I've been getting.

Jane You branching out into sex offence?

Rick No. Just the truth.

Jane I'm happily married.

Rick Was it ever happy?

Jane Yeah, once.

Pause. Then she continues, as if she is trying to justify herself

Michael was always different. Some said he was too sharp, but I liked it. Most guys are all front, but when you scratch the surface they are all soft on the inside.

Rick You think I'm all front.

Jane No, I think you're mad.

Rick I'm not mad.

Jane Then you are just a violent piece of shit!

Rick Is that just front or are you strong, Jane?

Jane We'll see.

Rick goes over to Jane again and leans close to her in an intimidating fashion

Rick Yes, I think we will.

Jane You don't frighten me.

Rick Because you like strong men? You get braver when I threaten you, don't you? You get off on it, don't you?

Jane Piss off!

Rick I think you want me to knock you about. It turns you on, doesn't it?

Pause. Jane gathers her coat, bag and jumper

It makes sense, Jane. I can begin to see why you stick with a husband who slaps you every time he has a bad day. I think you like it.

Pause

Well?

Jane Same old excuse for hitting women. I've heard it all before.

Rick But you're wrong, Jane, I don't want to hit you. That's Michael. I'm
   Rick. (*He backs off and sits down in the armchair*)

Pause

   So if it wasn't the danger, what was it?

Pause

Jane He was confident. He had money which meant we could do good
   things. He liked to risk his money. We went to the races one day and he put
   two thousand pounds on a horse because it was called Lady Jane.
Rick Romantic.
Jane Yeah.
Rick Did it win?
Jane Came in second.
Rick Each way bet?
Jane Yes. He bought me a Spider with the winnings.
Rick A spider?
Jane It's a car.
Rick Like the one outside?
Jane No, that's a Merc. What kind of bank robber doesn't know about cars?
Rick They don't interest me. So a Spider is what?
Jane Alfa Romeo. It's a sports car.
Rick Very nice. Lucky man, your husband. Inherits a lot of money, wins
   risky bets, marries a beautiful woman. Did your family like him?
Jane They came to the wedding.
Rick White?
Jane Yes.
Rick Nice.
Jane Money is money after all.
Rick And you can tell, can't you?

Pause

Jane What do you want?
Rick I want you to want to stay and talk to me.
Jane When you won't let me leave?
Rick I want to keep you here until you want to stay.
Jane Because you fancy me?
Rick No.
Jane You don't fancy me?
Rick Oh, yes, I do. Very much, but that's beside the point.

Jane How will you know?

Rick What?

Jane Whether I will want to stay or not.

Rick I'll give you the opportunity to leave.

Jane When?

Rick When I know you'll stay.

Jane Jesus.

Rick Don't worry about it.

Jane I know you think this is quite normal. But I find it rather odd to be trapped in a room with a bank robber who wants to be Britain's number one most wanted criminal, who forces me to stay with him and promises me freedom when I promise not to accept it. Sounds odd to me, Rick, it sounds bloody odd.

Rick I want you to help me.

Jane Why should I?

Rick Because we have a great deal in common.

Jane I once stole a tube of Refreshers from the local corner shop. I was eight years old and I did it solo. I didn't need an inside man.

Rick Well, that's a good principle. Never use more people than you need for the job. Did you get caught?

Jane No.

Rick You did better than me, then.

Jane No, not really. I was so ashamed I went back to the shop.

Rick You confessed?

Jane No, I didn't have the nerve, but I pushed ten shillings under the till when the shopkeeper wasn't looking.

Rick Shillings?

Jane It was before decimilization.

Rick I thought you were younger.

Jane Does that put you off?

Rick Not at all. I apologise. I shouldn't have mentioned it. Forgive me.

Jane Gallantry is alive and well and living in the criminal classes.

Rick Criminality is not a class matter. Lord Lucan exploded that myth. So come on. You left the money under the till.

Jane That's it. It was my way of satisfying my conscience.

Rick Why should that assuage your conscience?

Jane Because the money I left was more than twenty times the cost of the Refreshers.

Rick But what if he didn't find it?

Jane He was bound to move the till sooner or later.

Rick Suppose it was later. Decimalization might have made your ten shillings worthless.

Slight pause

Jane (*almost laughing*) Rick. I've overcome my conscience. I am no longer worried about the Refreshers.

Rick Good. That's an important lesson. Time helps you get over crime.

Jane Why do you say that?

Rick Because I'm a head hunter.

Jane I thought you were going straight.

Rick I never said that.

Jane You did.

Rick No, I said I had a clean sheet.

Jane So you're still in business.

Rick Very much so.

Jane What has this got to do with me?

Rick Can't you guess?

Jane You want me to ride shot gun for your next job?

Rick I want you to help me.

Pause

Jane You are mad.

Rick Perhaps.

Jane Rick, I don't have a gun. I don't work for a security firm. I don't need any money.

Rick (*with a smile*) Except for groceries.

Jane Except for groceries.

Rick Not all crimes are committed for money.

Jane For love?

Rick Or sex.

Pause

For money. For love, hate. For kicks. Revenge. For power. Crime needn't be about money.

Jane I don't want to be a criminal.

Rick Why not? Conscience?

Pause. Rick goes over and unlocks the door

Well, that's that then. It was nice meeting you, Jane. I hope you sort out your marriage.

Pause

Jane What?

Rick That looks like it.
Jane I can go.
Rick Certainly.
Jane This isn't a joke. You aren't going to suddenly slam the door again and make me stay?
Rick Not this time.
Jane I'm free to go.
Rick Yes.
Jane What about, "you hope I will stay", is that still true?
Rick Yes.
Jane But if I choose to go, I can go?
Rick Yes.

She hovers uncertainly by the door

Jane You ask me to participate in a crime. You don't tell me what that crime is, you don't tell me what's in it for me, then you say I can go. You think that's enough to keep me here after the way you frightened me?
Rick Intriguing, isn't it?
Jane I'm frightened to go. (*She pauses*) If you stop me...
Rick I won't stop you. (*He sits, as if to confirm this*)

Jane hurries out

(*Calling to her retreating back*) Don't forget your mace.

She closes the door behind her. He sits very still, then lights a match. The phone starts to ring. It startles him momentarily, then he ignores it. He burns the match through as before. The phone stops ringing. He finishes burning the match. Pause

The door opens cautiously and Jane looks in

He looks up at her

Jane You let me go.
Rick Yes.
Jane Why?
Rick I told you.
Jane To see if I would stay?
Rick Are you staying?
Jane No.
Rick Fine.

Pause

Jane I'll send you that money.
Rick Thank you, but it isn't necessary.
Jane No, I insist. It was kind of you.
Rick No, it wasn't.
Jane What?
Rick It wasn't kind.
Jane Of course it was… (*She pauses*) I'm sorry about leaving when you said you were a convict. I didn't mean to judge you.

Long pause

  I'm frightened to go, and I'm scared to stay. (*She pauses*) Why don't you say something?
Rick You know where I stand. You have to make your own mind up.
Jane Help me.

Rick walks slowly over to Jane in the doorway. They stand very close to each other, one's eyes looking into the other's. At last he speaks

Rick (*softly*) This might help.
Jane (*softly*) What?

There is a long moment when it seems they must kiss. Then Rick pulls a purse out of his pocket and hands it to her and walks away. She is surprised at first. She doesn't recognize her purse because she is so thrown by the fact that he didn't kiss her

  My purse!

Slight pause

  You bastard!
Rick Oh?
Jane You lied to me.
Rick No. I stole from you.
Jane You lied.
Rick (*laughing*) I told you it had been nicked.
Jane You didn't tell me that you had nicked it!
Rick You didn't tell the newsagent you pinched his Refreshers.

She puts the bag and pullover on the table and starts to check her purse

Don't worry. It's all there, apart from the money for the groceries. (*He pauses*) I put the till receipt in the coins section in case you wanted to check.

Jane Now you think I'll stay?

Rick Probably.

Jane You arrogant bastard.

Rick Possibly.

Jane Why shouldn't I go straight to the police?

Rick Because it would be embarrassing, and you don't like them much because of all the awkward questions they have been asking, and besides, you have your purse back.

Jane I'm not staying.

Rick Have you understood the game yet?

Pause

Jane No.

Rick I see a beautiful woman in the supermarket. I fancy her. Her purse is foolishly balancing in an open bag. I squeeze past her and steal the purse. At the checkout I gallantly come to her rescue. You liked the look of me and you thought I was charming. We started to click. I know this because I felt it, too. (*He moves a little closer to her*) And now I find out that this woman's marriage is in pieces due to some ordinary circumstances and some extraordinary ones.

Jane makes a little start for the door

Don't worry, I won't come near the door. You can run any time. Have you guessed yet?

Jane I don't know.

Rick Because you are distracted by chance. By coincidence. You haven't realized that I planned to meet you. The purse was a piece of good fortune. I saw the chance and went for it. Otherwise I would have had to offer to carry your bags or something and you might have guessed long ago.

Jane You planned to meet me.

Rick Yes.

Jane To recruit me for your unknown crime.

Rick Yes.

Jane Why?

Rick Because only you will do.

Jane So the chat up…

Rick …was incidental. Pleasurable, but a sideline.

Jane Why did you ask so much about my marriage? About Tracey's murder? Why so much interest in it all?

In spite of his promise he does now slowly come towards her at the door

Rick Because I'm interested in everything your husband does. I've been
watching him night and day for the three months since I got out of prison.
Because I wrecked his car, because I set fire to his office, because I've sent
him twelve threatening notes and above all—because I'm the person that
forced him into killing his mistress. I know that he did it because I made
him do it. You are married to a murderer. You hate him. I hate him.

They are facing each other across the room

Jane So...
Rick So I want you to help me kill your husband.

The Lights slowly fade to Black-out

ACT II

They are just as we left them, no time has passed. During the Act the Light slowly fades to moonlight

A long pause. Jane is transfixed. Rick waits. They are quite still

Jane OK.
Rick What?
Jane OK.
Rick OK what?
Jane Let's do it.
Rick Just like that? Aren't you going to ask any questions? No little doubts?
Jane I'll ask questions. I'm just agreeing to the principle.
Rick That's the first time I've heard it called a principle.
Jane Look, you made a proposal, I'm answering it. What's the plan?
Rick I'm sorry, Jane. I was expecting to have to persuade you.
Jane You must have thought I would agree.
Rick Eventually, yes. But no moral qualms? No "I love him really" scene? No speech about the sanctity of human life?
Jane Sanctity is for saints. Jesus Christ, Rick, you asked me a question and I answered it with the answer you wanted to hear. Now are you going to make a proposal or not? I'm shaking like a leaf here, and if I don't do something soon I think I'll scream. Now tell me what's going on.
Rick All right.

Pause

You must admit it's a little surprising...
Jane No, being seduced at Tesco's is surprising. Being held prisoner in an ex-convict's house is surprising. Finding out you've been chatting to the man who has been terrorising your husband is surprising. Being asked to murder your husband is surprising. Saying you will murder him, that's not surprising, that's just my fucking turn.

Pause. She rummages in her bag for her cigarettes. She finds one, pulls it out, she looks for the lighter and can't find it

Light me.

Rick gets out the matches and lights her cigarette. He says nothing

So are we partners?
Rick Slow down…
Jane No, it's time to move.
Rick I'm not so sure.
Jane I'm in. Do you want me or not?
Rick You're up to something.
Jane We'll call it quits then.

Pause

A minute ago you wanted me to stay, but I suppose this means you aren't interested any more. (*She goes to the door*) I'll be seeing you, Rick.
Rick You aren't going anywhere.
Jane You threw your dice, Rick. You took your chance on a double six and now you've got it you're frightened of it.

Slight pause

You've been terrorising me and I've called your bluff. Now you better start telling me what you're thinking of, or I'm leaving.
Rick You aren't leaving.
Jane What am I staying for?
Rick I've got your car keys. (*He holds them out*)

Her first reaction is to check her bag

Jane You bastard. So all that stuff about being free to go?

Rick shrugs

Rick You could have walked.
Jane Leaving you my Merc…
Rick I figured you wouldn't want to explain that to Michael. (*He puts the keys back in his pocket*)
Jane Give me those.

He keeps his hands in his pockets and jangles the keys

Rick Come and get them.
Jane It's a bit late in the day for mating games.
Rick You think so?

Jane Do I get my car back?

Rick Sure.

Jane When?

Rick I'm just trying to puzzle things out.

Jane Do you have a proposal or not?

Rick I'm just a little on my guard, Jane. You'll forgive me for talking bluntly, but I thought I would need to beg you to do this job. So I'll just take things a little slowly for a minute. What reason could there be for you to agree so readily to kill your husband?

Jane You tell me.

Rick I don't know. The only thing I can think of is that you have thought of this before for yourself.

Jane Is that so surprising?

Rick Perhaps not, but it seems to me—and this is just conjecture, you understand—it seems to me a remarkable coincidence.

Jane Why? We both hate Michael.

Rick Did I say that?

Jane I know why I hate him. Why do you?

Rick I'm just in it for the money.

Jane A hired assassin?

Rick If you like.

Jane Then why does the assassin start work before he's been commissioned?

Rick What do you mean?

Jane The car, the office, the notes.

Rick Call it a free sample.

Jane Don't you think you should take this seriously?

Rick I do.

Jane So what possible purpose is there for warning your enemy…

Rick Your enemy.

Jane My husband. Why warn "my husband" of your approach?

Rick To encourage him into thinking that he's dealing with John Finch.

Jane He won't care who he's dealing with once he's dead.

Rick But by then the word is on the street that it's Finch.

Jane No, that won't work.

Rick But it will. We start the hare running now, and by the time he's dead the story is about that Finch has a score to settle. By the time the police realize it's a blind alley, the real trail is stale or dead.

Jane Like Michael.

Rick Is that meant to be a joke?

Pause

Jane You're not laughing.

Pause

Nearly. I nearly accepted your excuse except for two things. First, I think you could implicate Finch without taking such elaborate measures.

Rick Maybe.

Jane Definitely. Your dedication to this cover story suggests to me that you must be personally interested in your client.

Rick You're my client.

Jane Your victim then. Except now I'm asking for your services you're fighting shy of your commitment.

Rick I'm just being careful.

Jane You'd need to really hate him to do what you've already done.

Pause

Rick And the second reason.

Jane The second reason is quite simple … you are Finch.

Rick That's ridiculous.

Jane I'm not stupid.

Rick But you are wrong.

Jane Here you are bearing a grudge from the day he sacked you and beat you up and you brood on it and you think "what better way to get revenge than scare the pants off him," and then kill him. Am I right?

Rick Why not just kill him?

Jane I don't know—less satisfying?

Rick What does Finch use for an alibi?

Pause

Jane I don't know.

Rick All roads lead to Finch. If I'm Finch, I'm going to need a good cover story.

Jane You could invent one.

Rick Probably, but I'm not Finch.

Jane I just want to know you're being straight with me.

Rick I am being straight with you. I'm not Finch.

Jane So why pinch my car keys?

Rick I didn't know how you were going to react. You might have gone straight to the police. I've planned this for a long time.

Jane In your cell.

Rick You think I invented that?

Jane Why not?

Rick I don't joke about prison.

Jane shrugs

Jane Impasse.

Pause

Rick You think I'm Finch.

Pause. Jane sighs impatiently

Just nod me through this, Jane. We need proximity talks if we're going to get this moving again. You think I'm Finch.
Jane I said so.
Rick Did you think I was Finch when I asked you to help me kill your husband?

Pause. Jane nods

You then, without much time for thought, agreed to enter into a conspiracy to murder your husband. That's not too harsh, is it?

Jane shakes her head

So you felt comfortable working with Finch?
Jane Get to the point.
Rick My point is, Jane, that I'm not Finch, so it's rather ironic that you are seeking security in the thought that I might be. I'm Rick. I have been in gaol for ten years.

Slight pause

If it makes you feel any better I could pretend to be Finch.
Jane In any event, are you going to tell me your plan or not?

Rick goes over to the window and looks out. Pause

Well? Will you tell me?

Rick takes a long look at Jane

Rick OK. (*He fetches the briefcase. He puts it on the dining table. Then he closes the hall door and turns on the light. He opens the case, but he keeps the contents hidden from us and from Jane*)

Jane Why the change of heart?

Rick I didn't trust your motives. Now I think I understand.

Jane So you are John Finch.

Rick If you like. (*He pulls out a folder*)

Jane What's that?

Rick This is a breakdown of the ownership and management structure of M J Holdings.

Jane Where the hell did you get that?

Rick I'm thorough. I'm a pro. I know what I'm doing.

Jane What are you going to do to the company?

Rick Make some money.

Jane Oh?

Rick In return for one half of M J Holdings, I will kill your husband.

Jane So revenge wasn't enough for you, John.

Rick I'm not… I think I will have earned it.

Jane I could probably get it done cheaper.

Rick But would you get it done right?

Slight pause

Jane Go on.

Rick You're tied to employing Michael. That's part of the original set-up. I suppose when you were starting off the business back in those heady romantic days, you didn't think it might come to this, but Mike covered his back. While you were planning honeymoons and wedding cakes, Mikey boy was drawing up the prenuptial agreement—I suppose the company was worth a bit more than a sports car.

Jane Just stick to the plan.

Rick You could try and sack him but it would end up in court. That's expensive and it takes a long time. However, if he were to die…

Jane I'd just give half the company to you?

Rick Correct.

Jane Sounds like the lawyers are cheaper.

Rick My way is cleaner.

Jane Unless we go to prison.

Rick I will never be in prison again.

Jane But what about me?

Rick Forget about prison. This is a team effort, I can't do it without you.

Jane No. I own the company.

Rick There's more to it than that.

Jane Go on.

Rick This paper, which you will sign, appoints me as managing director of M J Holdings. It's my contract of employment. (*He passes her the contract*)

Jane Congratulations.

Rick Thank you.

Jane Won't the police want to ask you questions?

Rick Why? You aren't appointing me for another six months. The police should have moved on by then. This contract is dated six months ahead. (*He points it out to her*) This is the advertisement you'll place next month for an experienced manager. This is my CV which shows how suitable I am. You'll interview me, and in due course you'll appoint me.

Jane (*looking at his CV*) My, you have done well.

Rick I wouldn't want you to hire any old trash.

Jane Hadn't I better sign it after the interview?

Rick I think it's better if you sign it now. Then I know where I stand.

Jane So in six months, you're manager. When do you get ownership?

Rick In three years time, I'm going to buy into the company. This is a record of the deal we're going to sign. Though once again, I think we'll sign it now. It's all above board and fits in with your charter's requirement.

Jane Where's all this money coming from?

Rick We'll lose it in the accounts.

Jane That's a lot of bad accounting.

Rick That's a lot of good accounting. We just arrange for M J to lose a lot of money in the next three years and I'll buy in with that.

Jane Just like that.

Rick Just like that.

Jane So the police don't need to know you exist.

Rick I won't even be on the scene when they investigate the murder.

Jane What about your fictitious CV?

Rick Why should they be interested in me?

Jane Your criminal record.

Rick They should be long gone by then. These documents won't even exist until after the investigation has died down.

Jane How are we going to kill him?

Rick Don't worry about that.

Jane I do worry.

Rick I'll take care of it. I'll make it look like a mugging gone wrong. They'll talk to Finch and they'll talk to you, then they'll forget about it.

Jane Why? They talk to Finch and they talk to me.

Rick If you need proof that I'm not Finch this is it. I guarantee they won't be talking to me. I'm not Finch.

Jane What are you up to?

Rick Trying to organise this deal. Now forget about Finch. He's a useful blind to distract the police, nothing more. He was a handy person to have to point the finger at when I did the office and the car…

Jane You said that…

Rick Jane, time is running out.

Jane (*rising*) You said that you did the car and the office so as to set up the false trail for the police.

Rick Sure.

Jane That's not what you just said. You said he was a handy person to point the finger at. Implying that you were going to do that anyway.

Rick Let's not play at semantics.

Jane I'm not playing anything. This is a murder you're asking me to get involved in. I know nothing about you. I think you're Finch. You keep denying it. The story you're telling me is full of contradictions. There's a lot at stake here. I think I'll play semantics, pedantics and any other bloody antics I want until I'm happy that you haven't turned up here just to bugger up my life. Now what is going on? Do you know Michael from before?

Pause

Rick Yes.

Jane So you have a personal involvement?

Rick Yes.

Jane So does John Finch.

Rick Forget about Finch. I am, I'm not, who bloody knows? I'm not about to spell out my whole life until you sign these papers. All right? If you want to hear it, you can enlist my services, sign on the dotted line. Kiss and tell— you can hear the whole sordid story. I'll say this, you'll learn a lot about Michael, and I don't think it'll make you feel any better about him. Now will you sign the paper?

Jane Then the deal is set?

Rick Yes.

Jane begins to read through the contract and shares agreement

Jane (*without looking up from her papers, quietly*) When?

Rick Today.

Jane (*suddenly standing up*) Oh God.

Rick It's best not to brood.

Jane But…

Rick Strike while the iron's hot.

Jane No, I need to think.

Rick You didn't need long to think about the "principle" as you called it.

Jane But today!

Rick Today, tomorrow, next week it'll still be murder.

Jane But to kill someone.

Rick Is easy.

Jane But…

Rick Why the cold feet all of a sudden?

Jane Today!

Rick Jane, you'll be free. Your conscience is a worthless handicap.

Jane Easy to say if you've never had one.

Rick It's like your appendix.

Jane What?

Rick It gives you nothing but pain. You don't fancy the operation but when you cut it out you get along fine.

Jane I don't know.

Rick You got over the Refreshers.

Jane makes as if to speak but Rick keeps going

Sign the paper.

Jane I don't know anything about you.

Rick You know I'm an ex-con. I've told you my past for what it's worth. Ten years inside has taught me the ropes. I'm the right man for the job.

Jane But to do this…

Rick It's decision time, Jane. Yes, or no? The dice are in your hands now. Do you want to throw or not?

Jane I'll throw, but I'm not signing this until I know why.

Rick That's the deal, Jane, the papers need to be signed.

Jane Maybe I'll just divorce him.

Rick Don't mess about. If you were going to divorce him you'd have done it long ago.

Jane What's the small print on this contract?

Rick Read it.

Jane Yours, I mean. The one you aren't signing.

Rick What do you mean?

Jane I mean why the revenge?

Rick I told you I'd give you the full story when you signed.

Jane No. I need the whole story first or no deal. How are you going to kill him?

Rick Stab him, poison him, then set fire to him. It isn't important. Now sign the bloody paper.

Jane How do you get him here?

Rick Jane.

Jane Do you do it with me here?

Rick Sign.

Jane How?

Rick God damn it!

Jane Do you think I'm stupid? Do you think I have no feelings? I mean, do

I have to stand here while you do it? I don't want to see that, Rick. I hate the bastard, but I can't watch, I don't want to watch. I mean, for Christ's sake, Rick, will you please try and understand what you are asking me to do? How are you going to do it? Why are you doing it? It's not so much to ask. I need to know, do I have to watch? Do I have to do anything? (*She becomes almost hysterical*) You want me to sign up for this and I don't even know what I have to do. Just help me out here, Rick, help me.

Rick comes over to her and takes her by the shoulders

Rick Shh. No, no, no.
Jane It's a lot you're asking.
Rick It's a lot I'm giving.

Pause

Jane So tell me.
Rick (*almost affectionately*) You are a suspicious bitch, you really are.
Jane You know everything about me, I know nothing about you. Unless you are John Finch.
Rick If I'm John Finch, why is the name on all these bits of paper Stephen Richard Mitchell?

Slight pause

Jane Who's that?
Rick Me.
Jane Why "Rick"?
Rick In prison they found out my middle name and started calling me Rick.
Jane But your name's Stephen.
Rick Stephen Richard Mitchell.
Jane Why is everything so complicated?
Rick That's not complicated, that's just life.
Jane Why didn't you just say your name was on the papers?
Rick It only just occurred to me.
Jane You want me to call you Stephen?
Rick I don't care, I'm used to Rick now.
Jane This is strange.
Rick (*turning on the lamp by the sofa*) No, it isn't. We both want him dead. Let's do it. Sign and we can start the ball rolling.
Jane Where?
Rick Here.
Jane How do we get him here? Tell me how it all works.

Rick Then will you sign?
Jane It'll help.

Rick looks at his watch. Then he sighs. He walks towards the phone

Rick After you've signed. You phone Michael and you get him over.
Jane How?
Rick You'll think of something. Tell him it's about Sophie. That'll get him over.
Jane When he gets here…
Rick I kill him. Throw him in the boot of the car. Drive him to the railway, dump him at the side of the track.
Jane The police'll work it out.
Rick You think?
Jane They find people on the smallest clues.
Rick That's just the cases that reach the newspapers. You never hear about the crimes that aren't solved. Like I said, it'll look like a botched mugging. It'll get a nice low profile investigation. No-one will ever know.
Jane Low profile! He's already suspected of murder. Don't you think the police might find this mugging rather a coincidence? We need an alibi.
Rick You've got one. You… (*He pulls an invitation from his jacket pocket*) …are at this shop's opening party. "Startling new fashions" it says here, so you'll enjoy it. Here is your invitation. It's a big event that runs into a party in the evening. You'll get lost in the crowd. Stay for a couple of hours and buy something. It'll look more convincing.
Jane And you?
Rick I'm in Birmingham, but they won't question me.
Jane It'll never work.
Rick Of course it will.
Jane You expect me to take lessons in not getting caught from someone who has just been inside for ten years.
Rick That wasn't my fault!
Jane I see.
Rick That's irrelevant.
Jane I'll be the judge of that.
Rick Are you threatening me? (*He advances on her*)

She goes to meet him

Jane I just want to find out if the person I'm hiring is good at what he does.
Rick And what do you think?
Jane I'm only being careful.
Rick OK. Good. Caution is good. The van had too many people involved,

that's why it went wrong. This is just you and me. It's sound. I trust you,
you trust me.

Jane Up to a point.

Rick A point should be far enough.

Jane I don't have to watch?

Rick No. I'll do it.

Jane What if someone sees us leaving here?

Rick So what?

Jane Wouldn't it be safer to kill him somewhere else?

Rick Why?

Jane Your own place!

Rick (*laughing*) This isn't my house.

Jane No?

Rick You think I'd do it in my own house? These people… (*he indicates the photographs*) …they're on holiday.

Jane So you broke in?

Rick Yes.

Jane We are standing uninvited in someone else's house.

Rick Yes.

Jane You said you had a clean sheet.

Rick Breaking and entering. Don't be pedantic.

Jane Doesn't it count?

Rick It's right down there with Refreshers. Now can we get on?

Jane You said your TV had been stolen, but when I noticed it, you said they'd stolen your laptop.

Rick I had to improvise round your suspicions. I couldn't just come right out and say "By the way will you help me kill your husband?" I had to see how the land lay.

Jane And the door?

Rick For Christ's sake, Jane, this is not a bloody coffee morning! I broke in. I lied to you. I'm terribly sorry. Now sign the paper.

Jane I'm signing nothing. You can take my word for it. I'm implicated in the killing anyway. We share the guilt. You'll have to trust me.

Rick goes to the phone

Rick I need it signed.

Jane What's the point? You're hardly going to take me to court if I refuse to pay up. "Well, m'lud, she promised to pay if I killed her husband." So what's the point?

Rick So what's it to you, then? Sign the bloody thing.

Pause

Jane (*sitting by the phone*) I'm not signing that paper as a protection against you double crossing me. I will ring Michael and tell him to come over here. I'll tell him Sophie's at a friends house and he needs to meet me there.

Rick Why would he drop everything?

Jane I'll say she's broken something, a valuable antique clock, and her friend's father is getting upset. Agreed?

Rick Then you sign.

Jane says nothing

Damn! All right.

Pause. Jane picks up the phone and dials

Jane (*into the phone*) Hello, Sally? … It's Jane. Can you put me through to Michael? … I don't care, I have to speak to him now. … Now. (*She pauses. To Rick*) What's the address?

Rick (*turning*) Elmwood, South Side.

Jane Hi. It's me. … No it is very important. … I don't care if you are in a meeting. … Yes, I guarantee it is. I need you to come over here. It won't wait. … I need you here as soon as you can. … Elmwood, South Side. … Listen to me, will you? It's about Sophie. … Yes … she's broken this clock and everyone's a bit upset. You'd better bring some money … and there's someone here who knows you… Stephen Mitchell, he's…

At the mention of his name, Rick leaps forward and grabs the phone—hurling it away from her. He twists Jane's arm behind her back and interrogates her

Rick What the bloody hell are you doing?

Jane Jesus Christ!

Rick Why did you mention my name? Shit.

Jane I wanted to find out if Stephen Mitchell was your real name.

Rick (*still very angry*) Now what do you think?

Jane It's your name.

Rick Great, that knowledge could cost you! Damn it, Jane, I thought we had a deal.

Jane We agreed to bring Michael over here…

Rick Not like this. (*He throws Jane on to the sofa*) Now he knows exactly what to expect. Now he'll be ready. (*He goes quickly to his briefcase and pulls out a revolver. He points the gun at Jane*) You've messed this up, Jane. With or without that signature I'll kill you if necessary. I've waited too long to mess this up. You've made a bad mistake, but I'll have Michael anyway, and if I have to have you too then I don't care. I don't care. Do you understand me? Do you?

Jane nods. Rick looks anxiously about the room. He locks the garden door.
Then he goes to the hall door and locks that, leaving the key in the inside lock.
He turns off the main light. The only light is the standard lamp by the sofa

How long do you think it will take him to get over here?

Jane stares at him, terrified, uncertain what to say

Tell me! Five minutes, ten?

Jane Ten.

Rick OK. Ten. OK. Now he'll have to break in. He'll try and come through the door. I suppose he'll shoot the lock off, then fire off a couple of shots to frighten me … then he'll see you there, that'll distract him, so the best place for me is here. (*He presses himself against the wall out of sight of the door*) No, no, because he'll already have seen you through the window. (*He closes the blinds all round the room*)

Jane What are you doing?

Rick Shut up.

There is a long tense pause while Rick surveys his preparations

Jane What's going on?

Rick Fuck it. I should have brought a shotgun. Does he have a shotgun?

Jane Michael?

Rick Of course Michael. Jesus!

Jane He doesn't have a gun.

Rick Of course he has a gun.

Jane No.

Rick He's better at this than I am. (*He turns off the lamp by the sofa*) Get up.

Jane gets up and Rick pulls a chair over c for her to sit in

Yes, I think it's better if he almost trips over you when he comes in. Sit down. Don't you move. This is good. (*He directs a wall spotlight at Jane's chair*)

Apart from the natural moonlight coming through the blinds, it is the only light on the stage

Jane What is happening?

Rick We're waiting for Michael to try to kill us. I may have to kill him first.

Jane I thought that was the plan, partner.

Rick Not like this.

Jane You want to gloat.
Rick Yes, I want to gloat. So should you.

Pause

Jane I don't understand.
Rick Shut up.
Jane If you were prepared to do this—pull guns and stuff—you must want this pretty badly.
Rick Maybe.
Jane Why did you let me go?
Rick I wanted you to sign the paper. I still do, but we might have to deal with Michael first.
Jane You just let me walk away.
Rick I knew you'd come back.
Jane You had the car keys.
Rick You'd have come back anyway.
Jane You couldn't have known that.

Rick shrugs and sits

   You took a chance.
Rick Nothing good comes without risk.
Jane Very profound. You got that from a Dartmoor Christmas cracker I suppose?

Another long pause. Rick burns a match

   Why do you do that?
Rick Shut up.
Jane You're going to shoot me for asking you a question?
Rick If I have to.

Slight pause

Jane So why do you?
Rick It reminds me.
Jane What of?
Rick My resolution.
Jane What resolution?
Rick Will you please be quiet?

A long pause

Jane Rick. I know you believe all this but I don't think Michael is the person
you think.

Rick What?

Jane I mean guns.

Rick You think he only goes into violence with fists?

Jane Well, why not? He's all anger. When he's not angry…

Rick Don't go soft on me. This is the man who murdered your friend Tracey.

Jane No.

Rick Of course he did, but you can't handle it. Well, I'm sorry, Jane, the ball
is rolling down the hill now. There's no way out.

Jane He didn't kill Tracey.

Rick Of course he did.

Jane No.

Rick He's a born killer.

Jane I don't think so.

Rick Don't tell me I did it because I know I didn't. Just as I know that he did.

Jane But he didn't.

Rick You don't know that.

Jane I do.

Rick How?

Jane Because I killed her.

Rick is astonished. He crosses over to Jane. Pause

Rick You killed her.

Jane Yes.

Rick She was your friend.

Jane She betrayed me. We've been friends for five years. For three of them
she was sleeping with him.

Rick I don't believe it.

Jane Why? Think you've cornered the market in vengeance?

Rick No, I drove him to it… He's such a violent piece of shit he cracked when
he got the last note.

Jane What note?

Rick I said that Tracey was having an affair with Finch.

Jane I notice you didn't send me a note.

Rick What do you mean?

Jane To tell me Michael was sleeping with her.

Rick An oversight. How did you find out?

Jane Just a normal way.

Rick What's normal?

Jane He was meant to be at a conference in Paris. When I rang Tracey's
office her secretary was off. I spoke to a temp. She said Tracey was in Paris

too. I was surprised but I didn't think anything of it. She hadn't told me she was going, but I assumed they were both at the same do. When I spoke to Tracey a couple of days later, she told me she'd been in Sheffield. The temp didn't know to lie to me. Tracey's secretary had obviously been lying to me for years.

Rick So you just went round and stabbed her?

Jane No. I sat at home all day. I didn't know what to do. All the misery of this marriage just piled up in front of me and the only thing I thought I had left was Michael's faithfulness. It was always very convincing, and now even that was gone. I got more and more depressed. In the evening, Michael wasn't home when he said he'd be. I got in the car and drove to Tracey's. I just left Sophie asleep in her room—the perfect mother. I thought I'd surprise them in bed together. Michael wasn't there. I confronted Tracey. We argued. She admitted what she'd done but she showed no remorse.

Rick And you killed her.

Jane I wouldn't have done it. I didn't want to do it. If she'd have been at all sorry…

Slight pause

Afterwards it felt almost like an accident. Even now I can't remember actually doing it. I remember shouting at her, then I remember dropping the knife and washing my hands. Then I remember all the cleaning up … until I decided just to leave. I just walked out and left her bloodied body on the floor.

Pause

Rick The newspaper said she was in bed.

Slight pause

"Bloody sheets".

Jane No. I tried to wrap her in a sheet. I thought I was going to get rid of the body. In the end I just wiped my fingerprints off the knife and walked away.

Rick And the police have been questioning Michael ever since?

Jane nods

Jane So, you see, he isn't a killer.

Rick And you are?

Jane shrugs

No, I think he is.

Jane No.

Rick Perhaps what you've told me isn't true.

Jane Why should I make that up?

Rick To save Michael.

Jane Why should that save him?

Rick It shows he didn't kill her.

Jane But you aren't here to avenge Tracey's death.

Rick No.

Jane So there's no reason for me to make it up.

Rick True.

Jane You think I want to be a killer?

Rick You are.

Jane I don't want to be.

Rick I do.

Jane You are different.

Rick Perhaps.

Pause

Didn't you enjoy it, then?

Pause

There wasn't just a moment's thrill? An instant of pleasure when you saw her sin and your restitution come together in a blinding flash of righteousness?

Jane Shut up.

Rick No orgasmic moment of fulfillment. You did do it after all. You did kill her. I mean here am I thinking I was going to shock you with my proposition and then I find you've already done a practice run. Tell me you liked it. Tell me about it.

Jane Leave it alone.

Rick No wonder you took my offer in your stride, a hardened criminal like you. What is it? Cut a throat or two before breakfast, is it? "Excuse me, I must dash. I've just got to nip out and kill my husband's mistress … no, officer, I didn't really do it. In fact, I don't really remember it, just the bloody knife and a few sheets." I really misread you, Jane. I thought you were the victim, and all the time you were callously waiting to level with Mike. You obviously don't need my help. I'll leave you to look after your own carnage.

Slight pause

What was the plan with me? Please tell me. Before I put my cards on the table. What could I have expected? Did you just fancy a bit of rough? Wanted to do it with an ex-con, before you saw if he might help with your next murder? Were you hoping I would make all the moves or would you have undressed me yourself?

Jane Stop it.

Rick I'm talking about this new and unpredictable side to you, Jane, the side that stabs indiscriminately, the side that accepts kindnesses from strange men. The side that doesn't shirk from killing unwanted husbands.

Jane Don't be so bloody self-righteous. You're plotting a murder for money. I was settling an old score, a betrayal, a double betrayal, his and hers.

Rick Deadlier than the male. Or as deadly.

A noise is heard outside. Rick starts

Jane What's that?

Rick Shut up. (*He goes to the window*)

Jane (*jumping up anxiously*) Is it him?

Rick I can't see anything. Don't move!

Jane I'm not going anywhere.

Rick Dead right. He should be here by now.

Jane Perhaps he isn't coming.

Rick He's coming. Although … he could have gone back to your house for a gun. Maybe we have a little time. (*He moves suggestively towards her. He strokes her with the gun*)

Jane For what?

Rick For each other. A chance to explore this new side to your character.

Jane You still want me to sign that piece of paper?

Rick I suppose so. After all, I've got another lever on you.

Jane I thought you didn't believe me.

Rick None of it matters, Jane. We'll work together. We'd be free of Michael. We could run the company together. Maybe we could set up home together. Maybe Sophie would like me.

Jane It's my company.

Rick Michael says it's his.

Jane You know it's in my name.

Rick I don't care whose name it's in. (*He has a small spasm in his hand and drops the gun. He recovers himself, before Jane can do anything*)

Jane Your hand playing up?

Rick Yes.

Jane What's wrong with it?

Rick How badly do you want to know?

Jane Why?

Rick I'll tell you the whole thing. My hand. How I know Michael. Why I
want the company. Why I'm not John Finch.

Pause

Jane If you tell and I think it doesn't affect me, if I think it doesn't mean you
are trying to cheat me, I'll sign.
Rick But you're in no position to bargain. I'm holding all the cards.
Jane But you might drop them.
Rick Can I trust you?

Jane shrugs

The paper isn't the whole thing. I would like the money, but I don't really
believe I'll ever get it.
Jane So why all the fuss about this fucking piece of paper?
Rick Do you want to hear this or not?
Jane Go on, then.
Rick I've got holes in my arms. That's why I drop things. The prison hospital
patched them up fairly well, but you don't get Harley Street doctors in
there. Michael made the holes.
Jane Why would he do that?
Rick Why? Why?
Jane He must have had a reason.
Rick Sure, he had a reason. I had something he wanted. That's all the reason
Michael ever needed. I can't believe you're defending him.
Jane I'm not.
Rick You are.

Pause

Michael was my hard man.
Jane On the security van?
Rick You guessed it. He was already a veteran, tried and tested. He'd done
some good jobs. He knew his guns. He knew when to shoot and when not
to. He was cool. A good crazy—Michael Jacks.
Jane What?
Rick Sorry, Mrs Donahue, I suppose you didn't know. His real family name
is Jacks.

Pause

It made him difficult to find. But not impossible.

Jane But Michael…

Rick He changed his name. Haven't you seen it in his face when he slaps you about? He likes violence, he likes to make people hurt. He refines torture and he loves money. He tried to kill me, Jane, he switched on me.

Pause

Jane What happened?

Rick The job went off like a dream. The timing was perfect. The van arrived on the dot. Michael shot four rounds into the air and one into the windscreen. It didn't go in, of course, but it made the guards freeze. They'd have wiped his bum for him after that. We cut our way in with the chainsaws, jumped in the getaway and we were off in six minutes. We had a lock-up two streets away with our first change of car. Michael was out first, loading the cash into the boot of the second car. Jamie, the driver, was still behind me getting the last bags. Michael turned round, took the bags I was carrying from me and then he looked up at someone over my shoulder and … bang, Jamie hit me over the back of the head.

Jane Jamie?

Rick He doubled on me.

Jane Why would Michael…?

Rick Why? Greed, power, money? Sound like the Michael you know?

Jane Then what happened?

Rick When I came round there was an unbelievable pain in my wrists. I hardly knew what was happening. I was dizzy and I was trying to look through clouds of smoke. My hands were above my head and they wouldn't move.

Pause

I was sitting with my back against the door of the lock-up and it was on fire. Michael had nailed my arms to the door. The smoke was choking, the heat was growing. I could see the flames. I was screaming. Screaming at my arms, at the smoke, at the heat and the flames. I looked up at my wrists. One on top of the other, a great hooked nail driven through them. By now the door was burning, I could feel my jacket start to burn. I pulled at my hands. I had to thread them off the nail. It was bent up like a butcher's hook and I threaded my wrists off it. Threaded them off the nail. I could feel the metal moving inside my arm. I staggered forward. Tripped over something. It was Jamie. Double betrayal, shot in the head for his trouble. Michael saved the inventive torture for me. He was a good Sunday School boy. He saved the crucifixion for the king.

Jane Oh God.

Rick (*rising and checking the windows again*) Somehow I staggered outside, and I guess I fainted. I woke up in hospital with three armed cops watching me.

Jane Didn't you tell them?

Rick I don't grass on anybody.

Jane Not even a traitor?

Rick Not even on Michael.

Jane Not even when it meant ten years inside?

Rick Fifteen.

Jane You said ten.

Rick I made parole.

Jane I forgot. You're going to be a postman. What's it like?

Rick Posting letters?

Jane Prison.

Rick Don't brood on it. They might never catch you.

Jane What's it like?

Rick I'm never going back. I'd shoot myself before I'd go back. It's like someone has tied you to a tree and said "There, I'm wasting your life for you. Watch it sail by." There is nothing of value left. You live for your release day. Don't believe them when they tell you it's too soft—it drives you mad. Day after day of the same petty routines. A good day is a day when someone gives you a cigarette. A bad day is every other day. It's nowhere. No life, no place, no future. It's like being dead but knowing you're dead. It's the worst thing that can happen to a man.

Jane (*quietly*) Or a woman.

A long pause. He gets up and goes over to the window, peers out

Is his name really Jacks?

Rick Yes.

Jane Even the name.

Rick What?

Jane Even his name was a lie.

Pause

Rick Will you sign now, please?

Jane Wait a minute.

Rick Wait? I told you. You said you would sign.

Jane You said it didn't matter.

Rick I said I'd never get possession of the company.

Jane So why do you need the signature?

Rick I want him to think you betrayed him. I want him to think that you gave everything to me.

Jane Everything?
Rick Yes.
Jane Come here.

Rick goes cautiously over to her. She pulls him down by his tie and kisses him. Suddenly he leaps back, holding his mouth. She has bitten his tongue. He lashes out angrily. She jumps up and gets as far away from him as she can

Rick You stupid bitch. Sit still, don't move. I'll kill you now. Shit! (*After a while he calms down*) Why did you do that?

Silence. Jane glowers at him

You're mad! I could have shot you.
Jane But you didn't.
Rick Shit!
Jane I said I'd sign if I thought it didn't mean you were going to double cross me.
Rick So? Sign the fucking thing.
Jane I'm not signing that, it's my death warrant. It always was.
Rick Don't be stupid. I can work with you, Jane. I'm good with partners. (*He refers to the kiss*) I'll even forget this little moment. You're an attractive woman. I'm a straight dealer. We could run the business together.
Jane You said you hated prison.
Rick What's that got to do with it?
Jane You said it's the worst thing that can happen to a man.
Rick Yes.
Jane Worse than death?
Rick Yeah.
Jane So—after all he did to you, you expect me to believe that you would do anything less than the worst to Michael.
Rick What do you mean? (*He raises the gun more attentively*)
Jane I mean you never meant to murder him. The real reason for your anger in my telling Michael your name is that he'll arrive prepared. You might have to shoot him. You don't want to shoot him. You want him alive. Alive and in prison for the rest of his life.
Rick I'd still never grass on him.
Jane No. In your schoolboy morals that's the only thing you wouldn't do. So you need a new crime. Something that's going to put him away for ten years, or better still twenty or thirty.
Rick (*very quietly*) What crime is that, Jane?
Jane Murder. Murder of his wife. You mean to lure him here and kill me in front of him. I assume you were hoping to save me until then so that you

can derive what ever pleasure you can from making him watch me die. What then? Nail him to the wall and let him wait for the police to come?

He advances on her, backing her against the wall

Rick I badly want to nail him to the wall, but it destroys the illusion, Jane. The police would never believe he'd done it. But I bought the hammer anyway, and then I thought if I nailed you to the wall the police might make the connection with my problem a few years ago. Then they'd really throw away the key.

Jane (*scared*) You shouldn't remind them, they'd want to talk to you.

Rick That's good advice, Jane; let's see how we get on. (*He grabs her viciously by the hair and leads her back to the chair*) You're right—I didn't want you to know. There is no grudge here. Not against you. I just need a serious crime to make sure they lock him up.

Jane They'll tie you into it.

Rick While he's already under suspicion for one murder...? I don't think the police will spend too long looking for other suspects.

Jane But the hammer...

Rick Yes, that might be pushing it. If you behave, we'll forget the hammer.

Jane You admit the only reason I'm still alive is I haven't signed that piece of paper yet.

Rick No. The reason you're still alive is that Michael hasn't arrived yet. If you think about it, the paper doesn't really hold water. The police would check it all too thoroughly. I was hoping to keep you until Michael arrived and I still intend to do so. But you are a bit of a loose cannon now. I had hoped that we could face Michael as a team. I wanted him to feel the full weight of betrayal. His wife teamed up with the man he betrayed. Double betrayal. No, the piece of paper was just for his eyes. I never expected to get the company. (*He walks around her, occasionally touching her with the gun*) I wanted him to see how you had turned against him. If you were alive and he could believe that you had signed this of your own free will, that would have hurt him. I want to hurt him. I want to take everything from him. The love of his wife before she died would have been a nice touch. There was a stage when I thought I would have had it without question. I can't say I'm not disappointed but ... that's a nicety I will have to sacrifice. (*Suddenly he whips out a set of handcuffs from his pocket. He swiftly handcuffs her through the arm of the chair. As he speaks, he puts the contract behind him on the coffee table*) Loose cannon should be tied down.

Jane No!

Rick I would have been your partner, Jane. If you had signed that, I would have worked with you. But you chose not to trust me, so you leave me no choice. I don't like to do it. I don't like to be violent. It makes me sink down to Michael's level, but that is as it must be...

Jane That's all lies. You were always going to kill me.

Rick (*working it out as he goes*) Maybe not. I still intend to have your signature. Obviously, I can never claim my half of the company. No court would ever uphold it, especially with you dead. But at least I can wipe it in Michael's face. He doesn't need to know that I forced it out of you. I can make your body look respectable. I can tell him you worked with me before you signed. Perhaps I'll tell him you signed it after we made love on the rug in front of the fire, that would be a nice touch. (*He collects a tea towel from the kitchen*) I'm sorry, I'm going to have to hurt you. (*Suddenly, he whips the tea towel around Jane's mouth and gags her with it*) If you don't sign, I'm going to kill you. If you do sign, I'm going to kill you. So there's nothing to be gained from holding out. I say this so you will understand the logic. You are hoping for Michael's arrival, but I might have another ten minutes. In ten minutes I could cause you a lot of pain. Why not die comfortably, Jane? Without my nailing your arm to the chair. (*He collects the broken piece of wood from the shattered front door, two huge nails are sticking out from it. He picks up the hammer from the sideboard*) Will you sign?

Jane grunts loudly through the gag

It'll be a last gesture—proof that you hate the bastard too. I'll show it to him when I show him your body. (*He lays the wood along Jane's arm, the nails against her wrist. He raises the hammer*) So what do you want to do? Will you sign?

Jane nods frantically

Yes? Good girl. Now we both know I will never own M J Holdings, so darling Sophie will get the lot when Daddy is sent to prison for Mummy's murder. (*He undoes the cuff on Jane's right hand, securing the empty ring on to the chair. He fetches the pen and hands it to her*)

She grunts frantically and shakes her head

You're left handed?

Jane nods. He laughs dryly

That would have been ironic, wouldn't it? Me nailing the wrong hand. (*He undoes the handcuff, freeing her wrist but leaving the cuff attached to the chair. He turns to collect the contract*)

Jane reaches behind her for the mace which was left on the dining table. He turns back. She squirts the mace into his eyes. He reels away. The gun goes off and the spotlight explodes with a flash and a bang. Rick drops the gun as he instinctively tries to protect his eyes. Jane gathers up the gun. Rick is writhing on the floor trying to deal with the agony of his tortured eyes, but also groping for the gun

Jesus!

Jane Don't move. I've got the gun.

He freezes

Rick My eyes, my eyes.

Jane Fuck your eyes.

Rick I can't see.

Jane That's the least of your problems. Sit.

Rick Where? I can't…

Jane The chair's just there. Sit in it. Put your hands in the cuffs. (*She pushes Rick into the chair, cuffs his hand to the chair. She ties his other arm with the tea towel*)

Pause

Rick (*still screwing up his eyes in agony*) What now, Jane?

Jane I'm leaving you.

Rick What about Michael?

Jane I expect he'll find you here. (*She goes over to the garden door*) I don't want to bump into him, so I'll wait until he's coming in the front.

Rick You still hate him.

Jane Absolutely. Won't be much longer now. You see, I can judge it quite precisely because I know the guns aren't at the house. He moved them when the police started questioning him. He has a warehouse about ten minutes from the office and about fifteen minutes from here. He couldn't do it any quicker. We've got about five minutes.

Rick You knew about a gun.

Jane Yes.

Rick You lying bitch.

Jane We've both been lying, Rick. Why are you surprised? I've known your whole story since you told me you were in Dartmoor.

Rick That's impossible.

Jane (*collecting her car keys from Rick's pocket*) We discussed the possibility that it was you sending Michael the notes. But he said you were still inside. Even when I checked and we found out you made parole, he still trusted in the name Donahue to keep him safe. He really believed it was Finch.

Rick He was never too clever.

Jane No. Just as well he married me.

Rick If you knew who I was, why did you stay earlier when you had a chance to go?

Jane I wanted to know what you were up to. You were a loose cannon.

Rick Dangerous.

Jane Doesn't mean you weren't going to be good or useful.

Rick So you're in on his scams.

Jane In at the beginning. I know how much to trust him. That's why I own the company. He had just enough wit to find someone to invent the clause keeping him on as director.

Rick From one little double cross…

Jane We made enough money to start M J Holdings.

Rick You knew him then.

Jane Rick, I planned the whole scam.

Rick You greedy whore. There was enough to share.

Jane But more if we kept it to ourselves.

Rick He never mentioned you.

Jane I told him not to.

Rick You told him…

Jane I did the thinking.

Rick So all that hate was acting.

Jane No, that's true. He's going down.

Rick What?

Jane Yes, you can comfort yourself with the knowledge as you die, that Michael is going to prison for the murder of you. I thought he would go down for Tracey's murder, but that hasn't happened as smoothly as I hoped.

Rick You mean you planned to kill her.

Jane Murder isn't something to rush into, Rick.

Rick I'll tell him you killed Tracey. He'll grass on you.

Jane No. I've got his daughter.

Rick You wouldn't.

Jane Whether I would or not, he'll believe I might.

Rick What if he doesn't kill me?

Jane We both know Michael better than that. He's predictable. He tried to kill you last time.

Rick He should have shot me.

Jane He will this time.

Rick I'll talk to him and explain.

Jane After the campaign of terror you've been running? He's going to be pretty fired up by the time he gets here. He's going to be carrying a gun for the first time for some years—a pump action shotgun by the way … or maybe the automatic… He won't hesitate. He shot Jamie. Why do you think you'll be any different?

Rick Because he never shot me before, he wanted me to suffer.

Jane Even Michael won't make that mistake again. He wasn't this angry before. Remember—he thinks you killed Tracey.

Pause

Rick Why'd he get Jamie to betray me and then kill him? Or was that another of your ideas?

Jane Jamie never betrayed you.

Rick He did.

Jane It wasn't Jamie who knocked you over the head.

Rick It was.

Jane I never saw your face. That's why I didn't recognize you. I'd only seen you from behind, and that was ten years ago. When Michael was sticking you to the garage door, I was moving cars.

Rick You evil bitch.

Jane You shouldn't have mentioned Dartmoor.

Rick I told you too much.

Jane Yes. This isn't what I was expecting.

Rick What were you expecting?

Jane I don't know. Maybe … what did you say … a bit of rough?

Rick You're flattering yourself.

There is the sound of a car pulling up

Jane That'll be Michael. He has been quick. (*She picks up the mace and squirts some more in his eyes*)

Rick Aaah!

Jane Sorry, Rick, but I'm about to leave you alone. And I don't want to give you an advantage.

The sound of the car door in the driveway. Jane waits tensely by the garden door. She unlocks it. We hear Michael pace past the living-room window. When he has passed right across, Jane whispers

Goodbye, Rick. I'll leave the two of you together to settle old scores.

Jane slips out of the door, grabbing her bag and belongings as she goes. In her haste, and unseen by us, she only collects her coat and bag—the jumper remains

We hear footsteps on the drive to the front. Rick lunges to the door which Jane has gone out of. He manages through his blindness to find the door handle but the door is locked. For a moment he hesitates, then, still nursing his eyes, he turns to face the hall door thinking there might be some escape this way. But before he can make a bid for escape, a great blow is struck on the outside of the door. Hampered by the handcuffs and unable to see, Rick freezes up and awaits the inevitable. Heavy blows rain down on the door from outside until a panel of it splinters. The butt of a shotgun is seen knocking the rest of the panel free. A momentary pause: then two gunshots. Rick jerks in shocked expectation—then realizes he hasn't been shot or even shot at. There is a thump outside the door. Pause. Then a woman's hand reaches through the hole in the door and unlocks it

   Jane enters carrying Rick's gun

   Hello, Rick. Michael lived up to my expectations, right to the end. He brought the shotgun. I still have several bullets left, so I suggest you sit still. I'll shoot you if you make me. I didn't believe you when you said prison was worse than dying. I wanted Michael dead. I'll be calling the police soon. This is your gun. It killed Michael, so you had better have it. I'm sorry I won't be leaving any ammunition. I'll give that to Michael.

   Jane goes out into the hall and squeezes off three more shots. She comes back in and wipes her fingerprints off it

   Shot him five times. Your lawyer will struggle to justify that. There you are. Take it! It needs someone's prints, though I suppose you might have wiped them off. (*She puts the gun into his hand*)

He still can't see and takes it, but immediately pushes it away

Rick I know too much about you, Jane. I'll tell them everything. You'll be locked up too.

Jane Who's going to believe your ridiculous story? You're an ex-con. I'm a respectable housewife. You won't even be able to prove I was here. (*She wipes her prints off the door handles, her glass, the fridge, the beer can, the arms of the chair. Everything she handled. She puts all the small pieces in the Tesco bag: the plates, the glasses, the knife, the documents, the pen— everything. Her memory and control are devastatingly impressive*)

Rick They'll believe me.

Jane I don't think so. I'm going in a minute. I'll call the police. They'll find you. You won't get far with your eyes like that. I think they might find some room for you in Dartmoor. I'll keep my eyes open in thirty years or so, in case you make parole.

Rick You bitch. I'll tell them.

Jane You tell them what you like. You'll be needing these. (*She gives him the keys to the handcuffs. Then she picks up the mace tin and wipes off the prints*) I'll just give this to Michael. We don't want them wondering what happened to your eyes.

Jane takes the mace out to the hall, wiping her fingerprints off it as she goes. She re-enters to pick up the Tesco bag packed with incriminating evidence

Well… I suppose I'd better pick Sophie up now that Daddy can't make it. Goodbye, Rick.

Jane exits

Rick slumps forward, his head in his hands as he wipes his eyes. We hear Jane's car start and pull away. He struggles to the sink and washes his eyes. He then stumbles across the room, tripping over a chair. As he gets up, he finds on the chair Jane's distinctive jumper—forgotten by her in her haste to escape as Michael came in. He fondles the sweater, and sinks into a chair, his eyes still smarting

Rick It's a one-off!

The Lights fade to Black-out

CURTAIN

FURNITURE AND PROPERTY LIST

Further dressing may be added at the director's discretion

ACT I

On stage: Kitchen counter. *On it:* TV set, old newspapers, length of wood with
      large nails. *By it:* kitchen stools
    Sofa. *On it:* briefcase containing folder, contract, pen, revolver
    Armchair
    Small chair
    Standard lamp
    Small wicker chair
    Long window sills with stands for family photographs. Blinds down
      at windows
    Coffee table. *On it:* telephone and notepad
    Small dining table
    4 carvers matching dining table
    Clothes hook on hall door
    Keys in door locks
    Cupboards containing glasses, tins of food, tin of biscuits, and
      drinks including gin and tonic water. *On one of them:* family
      photographs
    Paper towels
    Cutlery and crockery
    Kitchen sink unit
    Fridge containing ice, cheese, olives
    Tea towel
    Wall spotlight

Off stage: Supermarket carrier containing beer cans, groceries, spaghetti hoops,
      spring onion crisps, shoe polish, hammer (**Rick**)
    Car keys, handbag containing aerosol and cigarettes (**Jane**)

Personal: **Rick:** matches, purse, watch (worn throughout)

ACT II

On stage: As before

Off stage: Shotgun (**SM**)

Personal: **Rick:** car keys, invitation, handcuffs with key

LIGHTING PLOT

Practical fittings required: standard lamp, wall spotlights
Interior. The same throughout

ACT I

To open: Late afternoon lighting

Cue 1   **Rick**: "So I want you to help me kill your husband."   (Page 38)
               Slowly fade lighting to black-out

ACT II

To open: Early evening lighting, slowly fading toward moonlight

Cue 2   **Rick** turns on main light   (Page 43)
               Bring up general lighting

Cue 3   **Rick** turns on standard lamp   (Page 48)
               Snap on standard lamp

Cue 4   **Rick** turns off main light   (Page 52)
               Snap off general lighting, retaining standard lamp

Cue 5   **Rick** turns off standard lamp   (Page 52)
               Snap off standard lamp

Cue 6   **Rick** turns on wall spotlight   (Page 52)
               Snap on wall spotlight

Cue 7   **Rick** fires gun   (Page 64)
               Snap off wall spotlight

Cue 8   Sound of car off stage   (Page 66)
               Swipe of car lights outside

Cue 9   **Rick**: "It's a one-off!"   (Page 68)
               Fade lighting to black-out

EFFECTS PLOT

ACT I

ACT II

Cue 11   **Jane** exits   (Page 66)
         Footsteps on driveway

Cue 12   Door swings open   (Page 67)
         Two gunshots

Cue 13   **Jane** goes into the hall   (Page 67)
         Three gunshots

Cue 14   **Rick** wipes his eyes   (Page 68)
         Sound of car starting up and pulling away